BREAKING MAD

ANNA WILLIAMSON

...... WITH DR REETA NEWELL ......

BREAKING MAD

......

THE INSIDER'S GUIDE TO CONQUERING ANXIETY

......

GREEN TREE

LONDON · OXFORD · NEW YORK · NEW DELHI · SYDNEY

GREEN TREE
Bloomsbury Publishing Plc

50 Bedford Square, London, WC1B 3DP, UK

BLOOMSBURY, GREEN TREE and the Green Tree logo are trademarks of
Bloomsbury Publishing Plc

First published in 2017
First published in Great Britain 2017
This edition published 2018

A catalogue record for this book is available from the British Library

Library of Congress Cataloguing-in-Publication data has been applied for

ISBN: PB: 978-1-4729-3770-4; eBook: 978-1-4729-3771-1

2 4 6 8 10 9 7 5 3 1

Typeset in Futura PT by Deanta Global Publishing Services, Chennai, India
Printed and bound in Great Britain by CPI Group (UK) Ltd. Croydon, CR0 4YY

MIX
Paper from
responsible sources
FSC® C020471

To find out more about our authors and books visit www.bloomsbury.com
and sign up for our newsletters

CONTENTS

PREFACE

Ten years ago, I found myself in the grips of a crippling anxiety disorder. Until then, I had no idea what that even meant, let alone how it was supposed to feel. At the time I was presenting a number one ITV kids' television show, *Toonattik* – a job I absolutely loved and valued.

However, due to a concoction of stress building up due to a tricky relationship, a pressured and extremely energetic job which required a smile plastered on my face at all times, and a general inability to talk about my feelings to anyone, I imploded. Big time.

I can remember the day IT happened as clear as anything. I hadn't slept for what seemed like months, I felt like a rabbit caught in headlights, almost drifting along on autopilot not belonging to my own body or mind, petrified with every move and decision I had to make ... even having to choose between 'diet' or 'fat' coke seemed like an exam interrogation ... it was like I was existing through a fog, as though I wasn't quite 'present' in anything.

At the time I hadn't heard of 'anxiety disorder' or 'panic attacks', yet I found myself feeling, as I described it 'weird', 'not normal', like I was losing my mind. It took about six months to get to what I now affectionately call 'meltdown day', but until that point of no return, every day, EVERY DARN DAY, leading up to it I'd wake up to a familiar gripping claw-like feeling around my chest, and a general feeling of dread, fear and loneliness. I. just. couldn't. shift. it.

A day of doom and unnecessary and unfounded panic lay ahead, and I'd just wish and pray for it to be over as soon as possible. I was emotionally and physically exhausted, and the best actress in the world it turns out – I mastered a perfect poker face while privately crumbling inwardly. At one point I even fantasized about crashing my car to allow me the sanctity of a hospital stay where the world could just go away and let me rest.

How sad is that? A 25 year old, with the job of her dreams, a loving family and plenty of friends, and yet I was an emotional and mental mess. And nobody knew, because, to be quite honest, I didn't really know myself. How can you open up and get help for something you can't really put your finger on? Something you can't *see*? This, I've found, is the whole issue and stigma surrounding mental health. This is where I, and this book, come in – to put a rocket up the backside of anxiety and its unfair and ignorant stigma.

They say you have to reach rock bottom before you can climb back up, and in my case, that was so true. It took all of my so-called 'coping' to come to a head for me to finally get the help I so desperately needed – but didn't know existed *until* I'd had my emotional meltdown.

I don't know about you, but for me, there's perhaps nothing quite as exposing or mortifying as crying in public, it's just so damn cringey. We have this oddly programmed mentality to not show our emotions for fear of being labelled 'weak' or it being embarrassing ... and it doesn't help when people seem to shuffle awkwardly and run a mile when faced with a weeping walrus. To be fair I am not a pretty crier – I seem to produce enough snot and general facial secretions to rival a tantruming toddler.

That day I was feeling frazzled with insomnia, anxiety, stabbing chest pains and a foggy mush of a brain. I dragged myself into the TV studios to record another high-octane show, when something inside just snapped, and the months of fighting back tears burst like a dam. And suddenly they flowed ... and flowed. All it took for this release was a simple yet concerned *'Anna are you OK?'* from a passing colleague. It was like a key had unlocked months of pent-up worry, frustration, self-doubt and anxiety, and wow, it felt good to let it just spill out.

Not initially, mind you. Being quietly smuggled into the back of a cab, and sent home until I 'felt better' felt all too odd and surreal. But the three weeks off work and talking therapy that followed (see box that follows), and some short-term anti-anxiety medication to help me finally sleep, proved to be life changing.

That 'meltdown' was a sharp wake-up call to learn what anxiety was, who I was, what I wanted in life – and crucially, what I *didn't* want. My subsequent journey learning how to counteract the signs of anxiety and find balance has led me, ten years later, to writing this book.

In the years that followed my 'meltdown', I studied and trained myself, in a mission of self-discovery, and now with counselling, life coaching and NLP qualifications in my toolkit, it's great to be able to share with you the anxiety-busting skills, tips and techniques I've tried and tested.

Myth busting: Types of talking therapies

Counselling

One of the most common types of talking therapy, and widely available. Counselling is a type of therapy that allows a person to talk about their problems and feelings in a confidential and non-judgemental environment. A counsellor's role is to listen, guide and assist in resolving any issues in the client's own space and time. A counsellor won't usually give advice, but will help explore, and find insights into and understanding of problems.

Psychotherapy

Psychotherapy is a type of talking therapy used to treat emotional problems and mental health conditions. As well as talking, sometimes other methods may be used such as art, music and drama to help the client communicate more effectively.

Psychotherapists are trained to listen to a person's problems to try to find out what's causing them and help them find a solution. As well as listening and discussing important issues with you, a psychotherapist can suggest strategies for resolving problems and, if necessary, help you change your attitudes and behaviour.

Clinical psychology

Clinical psychology is about reducing the distress and improving the psychological wellbeing of clients. Through their doctorate training, clinical psychologists have an understanding of a wide range of psychological difficulties that influence people of all ages. They are registered with the HCPC (Health and Care Professions Council) and are trained to use several evidence-based psychological methods of assessment and treatment, to support people to make positive changes to their lives.

Psychiatry

Psychiatry is a medical specialty dedicated to identifying, treating and preventing mental health difficulties. Psychiatrists are medically qualified doctors, which means, as well as recommending and delivering 'talking therapies', they can prescribe medication.

Neuro Linguistic Programming (NLP)

NLP is a talking therapy focused on communication, and how the dynamics between our mind, language and behaviour affect us. An NLP practitioner acts as a 'mirror' to reflect what the client is offering up, and will help explore and guide through any issues, feelings and blockages which need addressing, through a range of approaches and self-exploratory processes.

Hypnotherapy

See section later in the book on Hypnosis, p. 168.

Mindfulness

Mindfulness means being aware of or paying attention to the current moment, including your thoughts, feelings and the world around you, nonjudgementally. It is about experiencing life as it unfolds, rather than being in thinking/worrying mode. Mindfulness approaches have Buddhist origins and have been around for thousands of years, but more recently they have become available as a type of therapy (Mindfulness-Based Cognitive Therapy and Mindfulness-Based Stress Reduction).

Mindfulness can be learnt during therapy / with a Mindfulness teacher or self-practice with the support of many resources (e.g. online courses, books, videos). There are many ways in which you can practise it: formally (e.g. through regular breathing exercise) or informally (e.g. in your day-to-day activities, such as walking or eating).

Emotional Freedom Technique (EFT)

EFT is sometimes referred to as 'psychological acupressure', and involves using a series of 'tapping' techniques on certain pressure points of the body to release 'energy blockages' which might affect a person's emotional harmony, limiting beliefs and behaviours.

EFT is considered a natural, non-evasive, drug-free approach to self-help, and can be self-applied by using the finger tips, as well as by an EFT practitioner.

Cognitive Behavioural Therapy (CBT)

See definition on page 1.

Whether it's feeling **socially anxious**, experiencing **panic attacks**, dealing with **sleep issues**, anxiety **headaches, lack of appetite**, feeling **stressed** or coping with **PTSD** (post traumatic stress disorder), the need to **self-medicate** with booze, drugs or self-harm, **low mood or depression**, pronounced **aches and pains**, I have some top tips for you.

Some may ask, (and I'm sure have done), *What do you know? What gives you the right to get on your soap box? Why should we listen to you?* – well, the answer is, I've been there.

I've been the overwrought anxiety-riddled mess, facing a scary work presentation and job interview on no sleep due to hour-by-hour clock watching. I've had the sweaty palms and palpitations walking into a party feeling like a sad Billy-no-mates, wishing the floor would swallow me whole as yet another mammoth panic attack takes hold. I've felt I was choking, been incapable of swallowing, and suffered horrific headaches due to the physically debilitating effects of anxiety. I've sought solace in one too many tequila shots just to get some darn sleep and rid myself, albeit temporarily, of the relentless anxious feelings. And, I'll admit this only to you, I've also called my mum in the middle of the night petrified, lonely, and crying because I can't sleep and *'need Mummy'* (I'm a 35-year-old married woman with a mortgage, and baby on the way!) ... so yes, my friend, I consider myself qualified to the hilt.

Over the past ten years, thanks to a brilliant therapist – I'm indebted to Dr Robert Schapira, one of the most talented consultant psychiatrists and mentors I could ever wish for – a loving family, supportive friends, a lot of self-acceptance, and a truck load of training and studying, I have not only learnt how to cope with my anxiety and panic attacks, but also to kick them to the curb and master how to not let them affect my life and future. I am proof that a mental health illness does not, and should not, define you, or even be a bad thing. In fact, I maintain I wouldn't be as happy or content now had I *not* suffered with an Anxiety Disorder. How 'mad' is that?

I am only too aware how many others have unnecessarily suffered, and are still suffering, from this debilitating and often life-limiting condition. Perhaps it's you, maybe a friend or family member. So a few years ago I decided to give something back – share the knowledge, so to speak – and I'm extremely proud to be an ambassador for destigmatising mental health, and a counsellor, life coach and NLP Master Practitioner, bringing my personal and professional knowledge, tips and techniques to as wide an audience as possible – through TV, radio and written articles, and also to my clients in my private coaching practice. Those experiences, and the feedback from the people I've come in contact with in my media work and my private counselling work, has driven me to write this book. It's my attempt to squash the stigma, talk openly about mental health and encourage everyone to take their mental health seriously. I hope between these covers you'll find bags of help, advice, support and acceptance.

When I was in desperate need of something, or someone, to help me, I found a lot of the literature on the market complicated to read, at times too full of jargon, and all a bit serious and clinical.

When you are suffering from anxiety, you are exhausted and on edge ... permanently. Feeling this way it's incredibly difficult to focus on a big read, or digest big chunks of theory. You want practical bite-sized words of comfort, support and help. A few tips and techniques to try and ease the crappy and debilitating feelings that anxiety can physically evoke. You need to feel understood, listened to, and above all 'normal' ... a controversial word in this day and age I know, but it's how you *feel* – take it from someone who's been there.

This is why I wanted to write this book. I wish this book had magically existed when I needed it the most. I genuinely believe it would have helped me a) understand what was going on; b) identify *why* and calm me down, and c) give me the mental and physical support, tips and techniques I desperately needed in order to function and to get help. And above all else, it would have reminded me that I was totally *normal*. You can never underestimate how important that is to an anxiety sufferer.

My wonderful clients, fans and followers often remark that they trust in me as their therapist and coach more *because* I have been there, than they perhaps would otherwise. That truly humbles me, and it's something I never take for granted.

Since starting my 'anxiety busting' crusade, my aim has always been to be 'real', authentic and transparent with my experiences and advice, whether it's on telly, in my writing or on social media. Anxiety and other mental health issues need to be normalised and talked about in a way that is real, truthful, conversational, without stigma, and even humorous at times – often, the best way to take away the power of anxiety is to laugh in its face!

I have dedicated much of the last five years to supporting the mental health charity Mind, who have been a huge help with this book; children's counselling helpline Childline; and young adults' charity, The Prince's Trust.

The Prince's Trust recently released a report stating that 1 in 10 young adults (16–35 years) are unable to leave their homes due to feeling anxious. And anxiety is now recognised as one of the major mental health issues in society, with 1 in 4 of us suffering from a mental health illness. It does not discriminate, or choose a certain race, religion, gender or social class ... anybody can suffer from anxiety at any time, for any reason.

Breaking Mad – The Insider's Guide to Conquering Anxiety is for everyone. It's for you, your neighbour and your colleague. It's for whoever needs a friendly helping hand. A 'go to', easy to read handy book to help recognise and deal with everything – from the first niggles, to the deepest depths, of anxiety, whenever and wherever it might creep up. Be it at home, on the bus, in the gym, or even the work toilet cubicle, this is your pocket guide for whenever you might need it.

Talking about anxiety can be the most terrifying thing to contemplate, I appreciate that, but it really shouldn't be. In my experience both personally, and as a TV and radio agony aunt and life coach, taking the first step to say '*help*' is the most empowering thing you can do. By picking up and reading this book, you're already on the right path – well done!

In *Breaking Mad*, I'll be sharing with you some of my personal anxiety experiences to help give some context and clarity, and tips and techniques I've personally used and developed with my clients, to cope with some of the most common symptoms, and typical situations in which anxiety can present.

So, help is at hand my friend, I hope you find this book enlightening, and here's to kicking anxiety into touch.

Anna x

Keep up to date, and get in touch with Anna via her website and social media:
www.annawilliamson.co.uk
www.lifecoachingbyanna.com
Twitter: @annawilliamsTV
Instagram: @lifecoachingbyanna

INTRODUCTION TO DR REETTA NEWELL, CLINICAL PSYCHOLOGIST

I qualified as a clinical psychologist in 2010 and worked in an NHS Child and Adolescent Mental Health Service (CAMHS) for nearly five years, before deciding to focus on my private practice that I set up in 2014. I currently work with children, families and adults providing psychological assessment, consultation and therapy in a private clinic in Bishop's Stortford, Hertfordshire. I am a mum to two young daughters, who have taught me a lot about human psychology!

My work as a clinical psychologist is about reducing psychological distress and promoting wellbeing. I do this by using approaches such as cognitive behavioural therapy (CBT – see box below), which is the therapy that I will largely draw from in my contribution to this book.

What is cognitive behavioural therapy (CBT)

CBT is a popular, widely available psychological therapy used to treat anxiety, and other common mental health difficulties. There is a strong evidence base suggesting it is effective in treating a variety of different anxiety presentations in adults, and it is recommended by the National Institute for Health and Care Excellence (NICE, 2011*). CBT aims to help people to change the way that they view themselves and the world around them. It assumes that people who are anxious have developed negative beliefs about themselves and the world. CBT is available on the NHS, through the Improving Access to Psychological Therapies (IAPT) programme, and privately.

CBT is not the only approach I will use, however, as I feel it is hugely important to consider the individual's context, which CBT doesn't always do. By this I mean individual differences: things like family dynamics, age, gender, ethnicity, education, culture and religion. These areas of difference can result in a real disparity in individual resources in coping with difficulties, as well as accessing support. So I find that it's important to contextualise anxiety and try to look at some of these factors when I work with clients. As an example of individual differences due to gender: men are much less likely to seek psychological help, but are known to make up the majority of suicides. This is a task for mental health professionals, to make sure we look for ways of successfully engaging men, so that their psychological needs are met.

As you are reading my sections, it might be that not all of the tips or ideas will resonate with you and your needs. This simply means that you are an individual: the techniques are not 'one size fits all', so if something doesn't work for you, don't do it, simply move on to a different idea/ technique which might work better.

My contribution to this book

Anna has done an amazing job with this book. She has definitely achieved her aim to be 'real' and transparent with her experiences and advice. I believe this book will be a huge help towards destigmatising anxiety, and I hope it will enable more people to start talking about their feelings and experiences. I admire Anna's commitment and resourcefulness, and believe this will be a valuable read to anyone hoping to find out how to overcome anxiety.

At the end of each chapter, I will share information about the topic from my perspective, and introduce my 'top tips' for tackling anxiety and related difficulties. My aim is to introduce a selection of tips and ideas which I find useful in my work with clients who are anxious.

Anxiety is a common mental health difficulty. It can affect us all, at one time or another, no matter what our background or circumstance. We all go through life events that have the potential to make us anxious, whether it is events at work or home, relationships or health, or life changes through parenthood or divorce, accidents and losses.

Anxiety exists on a spectrum – and we can all find ourselves on this spectrum – varying from a 'normal' reaction, to severe anxiety that stops people functioning within their day-to-day activities. Although it is useful to consider anxiety as a normal human emotion, it is important to recognise when it becomes more than that. 'Self-help' is an important part of addressing anxiety, but this should not be instead of professional support. If your anxiety is getting in the way of your day-to-day living, you should consider speaking to your GP or a mental health professional.

References:

*National Institute for Health and Care Excellence (NICE) (2011) Generalised anxiety disorder and panic disorder in adults: management. NICE clinical guidelines 113. Available at www.nice.org.uk/CG113.

UNDERSTANDING ANXIETY – THE *'WHAT'S HAPPENING TO ME?'* FEELING

Anna's Quick Fix SOS

CELEBRATE! Give yourself a pat on the back. You've just taken your first step to understanding and getting help for anxiety. Well done for wanting to find out more and for giving this book a try. You're already doing something positive for you.

PRESS THE PAUSE BUTTON Allow yourself some time each day, or week, to stop everyday activities and thoughts. Take some 'you time' to give yourself a chance to catch up on *you*.

INTERVIEW YOURSELF Ask yourself each day, '*how am I feeling today?*'... and before you respond on autopilot, 'I'm fine', answer yourself as honestly and openly as you can. Whatever the answer, react and take any action accordingly to ensure and reaffirm you are being the best you can be for yourself.

Breaking it down

So, let's get cracking. You may have picked this book up for yourself, or perhaps you're interested for a friend of family member. Or maybe you're just inquisitive as to what I'm going to share with you and how I want to help you. Whatever your reasons, I'd like to extend a huge, heartfelt welcome.

I know from experience how daunting it can feel to want to dip your toe into the minefield of 'self-help' books, but not *really* sure what to expect, and even more importantly, which book is the right one for you. I totally get it. This is one of the main reasons I decided to write this book. If you're after an honest, open, and at times light-hearted approach to this taboo topic, then you've got the right read.

When I was experiencing the deepest darkest throes of anxiety, I so desperately needed help. I wasn't sure at the time for what, as I couldn't put my finger on what I was feeling (other than it being horrendous), but I knew I needed and wanted someone to tell me it was going to be ok, and that a) there was a reason for how I was feeling and b) there was help available.

When you're experiencing any kind of mental health or emotional blip, the last thing you need is a big ol' bible of a medical self-help book, full of scientific terminology and jargon you can't fully understand. Often the last thing you feel like doing or *can* do, is read a lengthy diatribe of psychobabble. When you're anxious, or stressed, or depressed ... your brain and emotions are shot to smithereens, you're exhausted, the tank is running on empty. I found I needed quick, clear, easy-to-understand advice and help.

Just to be clear: there is nothing wrong with the more complex, traditional books on anxiety. Some are fantastic and they certainly serve a purpose and can be great for really digging down to the nitty gritty of neuroscience and chemical reactions in the brain. But I wanted to spare you the headache of sifting through that information for help, and instead provide a 'quick fix' guide for those everyday moments you might need a helping hand.

So, the aim of my book is to give you exactly what I needed all those years ago. Immediate help, empathy, tips and techniques on how to cope in the moment when anxiety might come a' knocking. I want you to be able to lead a normal life, doing the things you love, with the people you want, and understanding any anxiety episodes for what they are – an often misguided ingrained protection mechanism harping back to the dawn of time (more details on this in a tick).

Perhaps pop this book into your handbag, gym bag, briefcase or your desk at work ... you choose ... wherever you might need it to grab at a moment's notice. I've specifically designed the activities and chapters to be easy to read and jargon-free. Feel free to either work your way through the whole book at a leisurely pace, and/or flick straight to the pages you need to curb a pesky anxiety attack, stressful feelings, unhelpful urges ... whatever you need there and then, it's here for you.

So, ready? Good. Let's have a bit of an anxiety breakdown (ha, no pun intended) about understanding this bandied-about label – '*anxiety*'. What actually IS it? Before I crack on with a little bit of simple science and explanation, I feel I should first address a word I often use, and ▶

Activity alert

Rate my state

This quick and effective activity can be great to get yourself 'in the moment' and notice HOW you are feeling NOW. Why do we do this? When we give ourselves total focus, it can be hugely helpful in identifying our 'state' and what might need to be tweaked.

Get yourself a notebook, chalk board, page in your diary, your smartphone or tablet ... whatever is the handiest and preferred method to write things down. ◌ Either draw a line across the page with 1 at the far left-hand side and 10 at the far right-hand side, or write 1 to 10 (filling in the numbers in between) as a list on your device – this can be a good option if you're on a train or on the move. ◌ Now, take a few moments to just 'be'. Sit or stand wherever you are, and if you don't feel silly close your eyes too. ◌ Notice how you're feeling in the here and now. Not yesterday, not typically, but NOW, and allow that feeling or feelings to just 'be' for a moment. ◌ Now, if 1 on the scale is 'feeling great and at peace', and 10 is feeling 'unbearable fear and/or distress', rate yourself along the scale at where you are right now by writing or marking the number that corresponds with your thoughts. ◌ Wherever you have placed that number, ask yourself, 'what needs to happen to move that number down the scale by one?' – if you are on a 1, then that's fantastic, keep up the good work! ◌ Use and jot down on this scale each day and ask yourself the same question above, and notice any patterns that may occur, i.e. certain ratings on certain days, which might be particularly stressful or worrying. ◌ When we start to take notice of how we're feeling, we can start to explore how and if we need to change elements in our life, or what and how we could view things differently to get us nearer a 1 on the scale.

NB: If you scored a 10 and continually keep doing so, do consider contacting your GP or a mental health charity such as Mind for some more immediate one-to-one advice and support.

which you'll read at various intervals. That word is … 'normal'. Yup, I said the 'n' word.

A lot of people get very nervous about the use of the word 'normal', particularly when it comes to sensitive matters of mental health. Don't get me wrong, I absolutely get and actively promote being respectful at all times, to everyone, but just so we're all on the same page, let's clear this up now, the definition of the word 'normal' is: *'the usual, typical or expected state'*, it can also be regarded by some as *'a functioning level'*. Not for one minute am I being disrespectful, judgemental or anything remotely controversial by using this word, with the meaning I intend it. I often use the word 'normal' to measure how I'm feeling personally, so just to keep the PC brigade happy, it's important for me to highlight this particular point and get it out the way now. All cool? Great.

First up, I want to check in with what you feel is 'normal' for you. I tend to not measure myself against what anyone else thinks and feels is normal, we are all wonderfully individual and unique, and I very much celebrate that with my clients, friends and family. What my comfortable functioning level is may be vastly different to yours, so it's important to know who YOU are. This is the underpinning foundation of what I want to share with you – when we know who we are (and importantly who we're *not*) better emotionally, physically and mentally, it can be hugely helpful in kicking any negative feeling such as anxiety into touch.

What is anxiety?

If you're anything like me, the question 'why me?' will have been uttered more than once during bouts of anxiety, and any flutterings of symptoms such as the sudden blank mind, the sweaty palms, the thumping heart beat … well the answer is, we are all rather boringly normal. Everyone gets anxiety, in fact, many surveys have similar findings and the most general statistic is that nearly 1 in 5 adults suffer from anxiety in the UK. So with an estimated UK population of 64 million, if we take those official statistics, that means that nearly 13 million people are dealing with anxiety at any one time. Woah.

And if we break it down even further, The National Office of Statistics' recent findings (2015 report) suggests that nearly 20 per cent of the UK population over the age of 16 displayed evidence of anxiety and depression, and rated it 'high' as an issue in their lives, with the majority of sufferers, women (up to two thirds). Sobering stuff.

So, what does this mean for you and me? Well, firstly we're one of a very large 'anxiety club', and also it's a very common issue that is widely reported, so any feelings you may experience of loneliness and isolation, I really want to try and put your mind at ease a little that any feelings of anxiety you may be experiencing are felt several times over by others around you too – they just might not tell you.

When I first experienced my crippling anxiety and panic attacks, I felt like the most lonely and trapped person in the world. I couldn't fathom what on earth was happening to me, and I certainly didn't dare tell anyone for fear of being labelled a total 'weirdo' and 'nutter'... two words bandied about freely, but which can carry so much offence, personal meaning and stigma.

I remember the sensation of feeling like I was living my life through a fog, from a distance. It's hard to describe it, and you may have your own description, but I just didn't feel 'me', and I had no clue why. It was terrifying, and I truly believed in those fear-gripped months that I was seriously mentally ill.

But, I wasn't. Far from it, actually. You want to know the cause of why I was feeling so bad? ... stress. Good. Old. Stress.

When stress simmers

To understand anxiety, it's really helpful to understand about stress too, as both are closely linked. Stress is a pressure or an accumulation of pressures, which have built up to a level that a person can no longer cope with comfortably physically or psychologically. It's important not to measure yourself against anyone else, as we all can or cannot cope with things in a different way, and we all express ourselves uniquely. No one is right or wrong, stronger or weaker, it's just the way it is and should be respected that everyone is wonderfully different.

There are many signs and symptoms of stress, which may resonate with you. These can include, but are not limited to:

- headaches, neck pain
- difficulty getting to, or staying, asleep
- nightmares or vivid dreams
- irritability
- bowel or digestive problems
- low mood
- a decrease in appetite, or cravings for junk food
- indigestion
- feeling tearful
- feeling overwhelmed
- shortness of breath
- physical chest pains or flutters.

Can you start to see how stress is perhaps the 'warm up' act for anxiety? Think of 'anxiety and stress' as Ant and Dec, or Morecombe and Wise – they both fuel and inspire each other to work the most effectively, and they don't have quite the same impact if they operate solo.

Allow yourself to take a moment now and think about it, I wonder if the times you've been feeling anxious have also come hand in hand with a stressful moment or feelings?

To put this into context: I didn't realise it at the time, but back when I was teetering on my massive anxiety attack I'd been allowing various niggles and other people's stress to infiltrate me over a period of time. I say I 'allowed' it, because I unconsciously did. We have a choice to keep stress at a healthy manageable distance, or allow it to flood us with its effects. I didn't know any difference back then, so merrily my unconscious and conscious mind allowed every smidge of stress to stick to me.

I was in a difficult relationship at the time, we've all been there, and it didn't help that our work paths crossed over frequently so I couldn't have a break from the stress. To add to this, I had a high-pressured sought-after job, working with some other very strong characters. I was

Activity alert

Assess the stress

Either on a tablet device, piece of paper or a kitchen chalkboard, draw a 'spidergram' template (a circle in the centre of the space, with 'legs' or lines coming off it – like a spider).

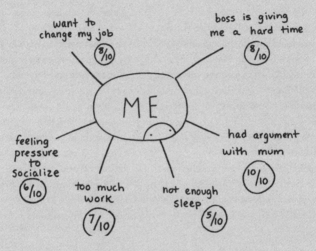

In the centre of the circle, write the word 'me'. ◌ Now, have a good think and brainstorm of anything and everything that is going on in your life right now, particularly which is causing you stressful feeling and thoughts, and what those feelings are. ◌ **As these thoughts and ideas come into your mind, write each one down at the end of a 'leg' on your spidergram.** ◌ Be creative and mentally scan through the different aspects of your life, i.e. work, home, family, finances, social ... and anything that comes to mind which has been niggling you and your stress levels, jot it down ... leave no stone unturned. Have what I affectionately call a 'brain dump'. ◌ **When you feel you've jotted down and offloaded everything that's naturally come to mind, take a moment to just look at the diagram, notice that it's now all out of your head and on paper (or whatever your medium) and allow yourself mentally to create some healthy 'distance' from it all.** ◌ Take a nice deep breath and allow any feelings of stress to melt away with the outward breath, and notice any

▶

pent-up emotion attached to that 'offload' taken down a notch or two – if it's on the paper, it's out of your head. ○ When you feel ready, take your attention back to the spidergram, and in this slightly distanced position emotionally, rate each cause of stress you've written down by grading it in order of importance/affected i.e. 1 to 10, 10 being the most important and/or strongest feeling. ○ Notice which have come out as the top three of most important reasons/causes of these stressful feelings, agree with yourself to 'park' the rest for now (they are still important but you can come back to these at another time). ○ With the three you've selected, have a think about how you feel about these aspects of your life, and what needs to happen in order for the levels and feeling of stress to ease. Do you need to do something differently? Talk to someone specifically? Take more care and time for yourself? Etc. ○ Just allow these thoughts to create and grow, and if you feel comfortable, come up with an 'action plan' of what you could perhaps do, or say or think, in order for the stress and anxiety levels to decrease to a more resourceful state. ○ Work your way through each point at your own pace (we don't want to create more stress with this exercise) and see what tweaks you can make in order to help yourself and ease off the causes of any stress. ○ By taking control back of the causes and triggers of these situations and feelings can be hugely effective in understanding what is happening and why – with the overall aim, eradicating any stress 'sirens' going off in your life.

completely at the mercy and control of my bosses – or so I thought at the time. So it was no wonder that chuck all of these variables into the mix, ramp up the pressure and expectation a bit more, my poor little emotional filter spontaneously combusted! Stress and anxiety: a beautiful relationship, when operating together they work like a dream and alert you to areas in your life you need to focus on more carefully – but they become a total nightmare when out of balance and you aren't noticing their effects.

So, firstly I want to explore your stress levels and check in where they are.

When anxiety is our ally

So, I think we're all in agreement at this stage that anxiety sucks big time, and stress can play a big factor in triggering it. But it's important to remember what it's actually there for. Anxiety gets a bit of a bad rap when you think about it, because without it as part of our built-in defence mechanism, we would perhaps walk in front of a speeding car when crossing the road, or forget to prepare for that important board meeting, or allow a young child to roam freely around a crowded car park. Anxiety has a job, and it's an important one too, the little fly in the ointment is when it fires off its signal at a time we do not need it, which can throw and scare us massively.

I wondered about whether to include this next science bit or not (not that there's anything wrong with science at all, it's brilliant, but just not the aim of *this* book), but for me, as a therapist who has read, studied and experienced a lot of this, I found it was the missing piece in the puzzle in understanding, and breaking down, a little bit of the 'what, how and why' of anxiety when it comes a' knocking.

I'll keep it as simple as I can, and hopefully it will help you in understanding a bit more about you and how your body and mind reacts to things – after all, they say 'knowledge is power', and I'm all for that. If we know how something works, we have a better chance of doing something about it and being in control.

Fight, flight or freeze

You may or may not have heard about the 'fight, flight or freeze' response when it comes to anxiety. If you take nothing else from this chapter, it's quite a good one to remember as it's a protective system we all have nestled in our brains as part of our genetic make-up, which actually dates right back to the dawn of evolution – a time when we *really* needed it to survive.

Let me try and put in to context: nowadays, we have a supermarket down the road, or an online service delivering your shopping each week to your door. We have friends, family and colleagues who are fairly civilised human beings (most of the time). If we have a problem or conflict with someone, the considered approach to resolution is to have a good chat, or even a good old argument if it's warranted, to sort out any differences – we certainly don't run around wielding axes and wooden clubs at a moment's agro – well, it's absolutely not accepted in civilised society, and quite rightly carries a hefty jail sentence.

But if you were a caveman back in the day, danger was around every corner. Imagine going hunting for a wild beast in the woods: your wits are about you at every moment, waiting for your target to come rushing out of the undergrowth, and the constant threat of a neighbouring hostile tribe about to pounce at all times.

How might that caveman be feeling? What would his physiology (body language) be telling us? It's likely his body would be tense, in a protective poise, his eyes wide and alert for signs of danger, his heart would be racing as the adrenalin coursed through his body serving as an extra boost of concentration and alertness, his breath would no doubt be shallow to allow more oxygen into the blood stream, and his body covered in a thin layer of sweat to cool him down. His bowels and digestive system would temporarily shut down to allow even more blood flow to other parts of the body where they were needed more urgently, i.e. the legs for running, which would also dry our saliva up. He would be physically and mentally 'aroused' (and I don't mean that in the 'snigger' way most people interpret that word) and ready for action ... either to 'fight' the animal, run away and take 'flight' sharpish, or 'freeze' to be inconspicuous and not draw attention to himself.

Once the animal had been caught, or the unfriendly tribe run away from, the physical symptoms would gradually ease off, reduce and before too long go altogether. What a brilliant and sophisticated defence mechanism!

Fast forward several thousand years to present day, and guess what, we still have the same response unit alive and kicking in our brains. On one hand, great; on the other, not so much. Why? Because that early-developed part of our brain cannot distinguish between what is *actually* life-threatening danger and *perceived* danger. To also throw into the mix, it doesn't know the difference between *real* or *imagined* life-threatening events – ah, perhaps not quite so sophisticated after all.

In a nutshell, our fabulous protective defence mechanism has a mind of its own when it comes to assessing what we should and shouldn't get anxious about. So, if for example you're sat at home *thinking* about how awful it might be to get caught up in a crowd, or how embarrassed you'd be if you forgot what you were saying in a work presentation – if we imagine it clearly enough, and the feelings it will evoke, we can actually give a very clear signal to that part of the brain to trigger the fight, flight or freeze response.

If we're *physically* in a train carriage or crowded lift, or your boss is hauling you over the coals for something, and we feel we can't escape, the same signal is triggered and stays switched on. After a time, if these situations and thoughts continue unchallenged by you, and are accompanied by a feeling of dread, your anxiety will exacerbate.

What we can do about it

Science bit over now, promise. I find it's always useful to understand the reasons something can happen in order to know how to combat it. The good news is we can do several things about looking after our stress and anxiety levels to keep them in check and at a healthy dull roar. Over the next few chapters I'm going to be breaking down the several symptoms that anxiety can present, and giving you 'quick fix' tips and techniques, as well as long-term suggestions, in coping with tricky situations, which I personally and professionally use.

This book is for you to use as a coping strategy for when you might just need an empathic ear in the moment anxiety is proving an issue. It's important that you also consider, should you need it, speaking with other health care professionals such as your GP, a counsellor or life coach, or a charity such as Anxiety UK, Rethink or Mind, who could also offer help and support.

Medication myths – 'to take or not to take, that is the question'

I'm often asked my opinion on medication treatment with regards to anxiety. As I am throughout this book, I want to be completely honest and open with you about my own experiences and feelings, and medication is one area I've often fluctuated on with regards to my stance on it.

When I was finally signed off work and diagnosed by my Consultant Psychiatrist with anxiety, he prescribed me two forms of medication: Xanax (Alprazolam), a benzodiazepine used to treat anxiety and panic disorders, proved a well-needed short-term rest from the frayed physical and emotional feelings I was experiencing; and Escitalopram, which is a common drug used to treat depression and anxiety, was prescribed for more long-term assistance.

Both medications were strictly monitored at all times by both my consultant psychiatrist (Dr Schapira) and my GP, which is key (these types of pills should *never* be taken without a programme structure or professional support), and under their care, once I'd had some much-needed sleep and rest thanks to the Xanax, and some time chilling, snivelling into a pack of Kleenex and watching copious amounts of *Friends* repeats on my parents' couch to quieten my mind, I was able to think more clearly to start working out the actual causes of my anxiety through talking therapy.

Medication is a huge topic, which has much debate and opinion attached to it, and I would urge you to seek out your own individual needs from a medical professional if this is something that is relevant to you.

Personally speaking, I am very satisfied with the course of action that was taken by, and for, me. By the time I was signed off work I was so emotionally wrung out that quick medical intervention to help me sleep and shut off the part of my brain flooded with stress hormones was gladly received. The initial medication of Xanax was removed after three weeks as it had done its job, by this point the low dose of Escitalopram had started to do its thing (it takes a good four weeks or so to really feel the benefits, even though you might not notice – it's a gradual thing), and so I was able to work through everything else verbally with my Consultant to reach a much more manageable state.

I have been medication-free for some time, but I have no issue whatsoever with going back on it should I ever need to. It's there for a reason, and so many feel embarrassed or stigmatised if they do the same, and it really shouldn't be like that. My advice, as long as you are doing what works and is best for you, and you're acting under the guidance of your GP face to face, rather than Dr Google, then that's truly all that matters.

Medication has its place but in my opinion, a combination approach of both medication and talking therapy can often be the most effective solution. I feel very strongly that all medication for mental health issues should unquestionably go hand in hand with a talking therapy such as counselling, NLP (neuro-linguistic programming), CBT (cognitive behavioural therapy), EFT (emotional freedom technique), or whatever is considered most appropriate or floats your boat more. If in doubt, always refer to your GP for further advice.

Finally for this chapter, I want to check in with how you're feeling and tweak you into a resourceful state and frame of mind to continue into the rest of the book feeling positive, inquisitive and raring to take control back from your unwanted feelings.

Activity alert

Play with your perspective

Have a think about how you *want* to feel – not necessarily how you're feeling now, although if you're feeling good this is brilliant and I want you to build on that even more. ☉ Separate yourself from any rubbish feelings or situations from the recent past which have perhaps, up until now, caused you negative feelings and thoughts, and allow yourself to picture how you're going to feel from now on. ☉ **Change any negative words or sentences you use for more positive ones, for example, 'I don't want to feel awful', turn into 'I'm going to feel relaxed and well'.** ☉ Keep tweaking the visual image you have to make it as appealing as can be, see yourself with a smile on your face in the sunshine, for example, and ensure that all words and internal dialogue are switched to a positive influence. ☉ **Allow these nice feelings and thoughts to just 'be', take a deep breath, roll your shoulders back, and welcome a more positive you.**

Dr Reetta says...
Understanding anxiety

Anna's experience of not initially recognising her anxiety is very common. Most people think there is something 'wrong' with them, some worry about the physical symptoms, others think they are weird or crazy. Like Anna did, many feel very alone with their experience. It is common for people to think they shouldn't ever have to feel anxious, and that anxiety must be avoided at all costs. Behind this is the idea that anxiety will damage them or make them mad. But as Anna says, anxiety has a survival purpose, so is definitely not a sign of madness or weakness, and, when experienced in the right balance, is not damaging.

I like Anna's 'Assess the stress' activity, which will give you a good understanding of what's contributing to your current anxiety. In my work as a clinical psychologist, I help clients understand their anxiety by developing a 'formulation' (an account of what's going on), which means we explore different factors that may be contributing to their concerns, including difficult experiences, changes or losses from their childhood and more recent years. Some people have always been 'worriers' (whether it is through genetics or how they were raised), while others become anxious following an upsetting event. I also explore what keeps the anxiety going – common reasons are: avoiding situations, seeking but not accepting reassurance, 'biased thinking', and good intentions on the part of others which help people to avoid the thing that they fear. As well as focusing on all the difficulties, it is important to remember people's strengths, so that they can use them to tackle their difficulties. Having a personalised 'formulation' or understanding of your anxiety is a very good starting point for addressing it. Anna has clearly developed this for herself, as you will find out when you get further into the book.

To understand and overcome anxiety: learn about what it is (this book is a great start), learn to relax, challenge your thoughts and face your fears. This approach is based on CBT, a commonly used psychological therapy to treat anxiety. I will keep coming back to and expanding on these points throughout the book.

Top tips for overcoming anxiety

1. *Learn about anxiety and that it's normal.* It is something that all of us experience at one point or another, so we might as well change our 'relationship' with it – and accept it as part of being a human. Anxiety is made up of three parts: thoughts, physical sensations and behaviours. Understanding what anxiety looks like for *you* will help you tackle it.

2. *Learn ways to relax.* As Anna does with her clients, I support my clients to practise calm breathing and muscle relaxation. There are endless ways of relaxing, so experiment to find what works for you. For example, adult colouring books have become a very popular way of finding calm. Other ways could be yoga, swimming, listening to music. Find out what works for you personally, to allow yourself to switch off.

3. *Talk back to your thoughts – also known as 'thought challenging'.* Don't believe every thought you think. Anxiety makes us view the world as very threatening. It is important to aim for a balance between anxious thinking and realistic thinking. There are a number of 'thinking traps' that anxiety pushes us into, so it is useful to remind yourself to develop and test alternative, more helpful beliefs.

4. *Face your fears and gradually work towards your goal.* Do this by making a list of situations that you avoid, and put them in order of increasing difficulty. This is called 'exposure' and the idea is that you remain in the situation until your anxiety goes down. It won't be easy, and it will take some committed hard work from you, but it does work.

As Anna says, working on any self-help techniques at your own pace is important. You can't hurry the process. Sometimes the first step needs to be a balance between accepting the situation (this doesn't mean you like it) and aiming to make a change. If you get this balance right, you will be able to start problem solving ways forward, while appreciating yourself as you are.

2
PANIC ATTACKS – THE 'FREAKED OUT' FEELING

It's important to remember that during a panic attack you might feel like you're going to die or you're going mad, but the good news is, you are nothing of the sort. A panic attack itself won't kill you, it can feel flipping horrendous but it won't win. It can last up to around 20 minutes, but only a few minutes at its peak, and can be triggered when you least expect it (those are the really scary ones that catch you off guard).

Anna's Quick Fix SOS

BREATHE Get your breathing under control – breathe in for 7 seconds (through your nose), pause, and then out for 11 seconds. This is the quickest way to calm any panic feelings down.

TIME OUT Find a 'safe' place: i.e. a toilet cubicle, the car, a quiet corner, and allow any horrible feelings to just happen and pass over you – don't fight it (it'll go away quicker).

TELL A TRUSTED BUDDY Confide in someone you feel comfortable with and tell them what you need in that moment (and what you don't).

Getting a grip on 'the grip' of panic

Welcome to the bit of the book where we get the lowdown on panic attacks. What do those words conjure up for you? For me, it's almost as bad as the feeling itself, and serves to evoke even more panic and anxiety. I wonder if whoever invented the terminology ever actually *had* a panic attack ... I'm inclined to think not as I find it such an aggressive and negative moniker. Although, to be fair, that's exactly what a panic attack can feel like ... a state of being 'attacked' by 'panic'. (I still don't think the name is helpful though.)

So, the first thing I want us to do is to change this label. Words and their association can be hugely powerful, and key to how they make us ▶

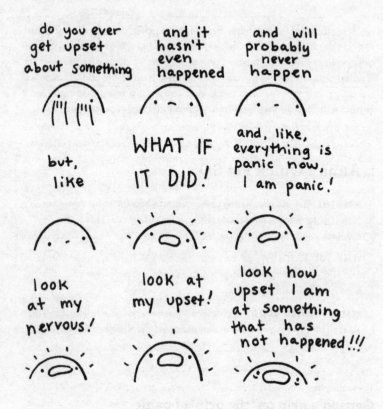

feel, both consciously and subconsciously. This is why I'm going to help empower you to take charge of a dreaded 'panic attack' and knock the power out of it, starting from the grass roots. The name.

What's in a name? quoth Juliet in Shakespeare's *Romeo and Juliet.* The star-crossed lover points out for us, hundreds of years later, that a name is 'an artificial and meaningless convention'. When it comes to the vocabulary used in the mental health arena, I couldn't agree more. 'Panic attack', 'post traumatic stress disorder', 'self-harm'...it's all pretty alarming stuff just by the wording alone, let alone the definition or how it can feel.

For me, being diagnosed with a 'panic disorder' and 'generalised anxiety disorder' was frankly petrifying, and more than a little dramatic with its professional label. So, the first thing I did – I changed it. ▶

Activity alert

Creating your own name

Have a brainstorm either in your head or on a piece of paper ... what do the words 'panic attack' mean to you? Write down or think of as many words as you can ... how does it feel? What does it look like? Does it have a sound or sensation? Perhaps it smells or tastes of something? ☉ Next up, either on a new piece of paper or in your head, have a think of some new words you can use to describe 'panic attack' but in a more positive, less negatively emotionally charged way ... i.e. another way to describe 'panic' is 'excitement' or 'adrenalin'. Another word for 'attack' could be 'experience' or 'moment'. ☉ Once you've come up with your new 'nicer' definitions, have a play around with the words and create your own, personal, new name for 'panic attacks'. ☉ Notice how it feels thinking in this new way. Has it taken away some of the power and fear that you perhaps experienced before? ☉ Keep playing and experimenting with the new words, until you come up with something which feels right for you. ☉ From now on, every time you hear or read the words 'panic attack' (and that includes in this book), I want to you replace the label with your new, more agreeable one. Boom! You're in control my friend.

Ok, so now we've taken the power out of the words, and just so we're all on the same page (literally), if I may, I'll revert to using the 'old school' name, panic attack (*insert your new name*) for now, just so we all know what I'm referring to.

I didn't want to 'be' the label I was given, and God forbid accept it and hide behind it as a lifelong excuse for people to pigeonhole and feel sorry for me. Not going to happen. When you take the power out of something, it can go a long way to dissolving a lot of the impact it has.

So for example, I changed the word 'panic' to '*energy*', and the word 'attack' to '*overload*' ... how much less scary is it to think of a panic attack as an '*energy overload*', it sounds almost positive doesn't it? Most importantly it really worked for me, so I'm hoping it might for you too. Fancy giving it a try?

My story

Panic attacks are really what started my journey with anxiety, they were my particular anxiety symptom, and my reaction when I was most stressed. Anxiety can present itself in many different ways, but for me, the first foray into this most un-fun condition was one massive, life-shattering panic attack at work. I best describe it as the 'freaked out' feeling, as that is exactly how it can feel. Totally and utterly spooked, weirded out, completely freaked. This panic attack which crept up and walloped my whole body without me even having chance to stop or understand it, acted as the green light for this response to happen whenever it darn well liked. It was like the floodgates had opened and now this beast had been released, it felt it had the right to crop up to render me petrified and useless whenever it so chose. The fear became the fear of the fear ... and then I was in all sorts of a pickle.

So, how did it start? I was presenting a popular kids' telly show on ITV at the time, called *Toonattik*, and I loved my job. I loved the team, the work, the show, the viewers ... it really was the best job ever. So why did I feel so awful to the point of having a total meltdown at work? Emotional stress played a huge part in it, which I've talked about a little in Chapter 1, but essentially, I hadn't recognised the physical and mental signs that had been increasingly nagging at me in the weeks leading up to 'panic attack' day.

It started building about six months beforehand, waking up each day, after a shocking night's sleep, with a general feeling of unease and dread, petrified about making even the simplest of decisions (even choosing what brand of fizzy water to buy in Tesco was enough to render me a gibbering wreck), and a foggy feeling about everything I did. I was worrying about everything and anything, and, although I didn't realise it at the time, I'd begun to get very obsessive about routine and timings.

In my job as a presenter there are a lot of long hours and last-minute changes, there are also a lot of big personalities and egos – which, it turns out, is probably the best combination to induce the mother of all panic attacks. I'd never before had an issue learning lines or being one step ahead of the game creatively, in fact I'd prided myself on it, however, I started to get increasingly wound up internally and panicked if my scripts weren't ready on time. It wasn't a diva thing (far from it!), and my producers, unbeknown to them what state I was getting myself into, had a job to do and were fully entitled to take what time they needed to get my scripts right. But gradually this feeling of unease crept up on me week by week, and if certain things weren't done by a certain time (i.e. my script given to me on time to learn my lines, my cab arriving bang on time to take me home to ensure I had a good night's sleep) I'd have a massive internal freak out! It wasn't anyone's fault, it was my body's way of warning me that something was about to give... It was like a wind-up toy getting wound, and wound, to the point it couldn't be wound any more, and the burst of release was the only action left. My perspective and rational thinking was gradually becoming more and more distorted as I began to place bigger conditions and demands on myself, and my now obsessive compulsive thinking.

How many of us have had restrictive and unhelpful thoughts such as, *'if I don't get to sleep by 10pm, I won't have enough energy to see the next day through'* etc. Well, during this gradual process, I was doing this with *every* thought for *every* action, and you can imagine the stress I was putting myself under. And what happens when you place these demands on oneself? The result is totally counterproductive, as you've given a clear signal to your brain to do the complete opposite of what you fear. The brain does not process negatives, so all it would hear in that instance is *'don't get to sleep, I won't have enough energy'*. I look back now and think 'NO ANNA', but I didn't know all I do now, so I learnt the hard way unfortunately – something I don't want you to have to do if it can be helped.

Those weekly, which turned to daily, freak outs one day manifested into an internal mental 'explosion', which, quite simply, scared the living daylights out of me. I'd never heard of panic attacks, let alone knew what they felt like, what they were or how to stop them. Certainly nobody spoke of them publicly or in conversation to my knowledge. All I felt was the biggest head case and as though something was seriously, *seriously* wrong with me.

When panic attacked

It's actually quite hard to write this bit, as it evokes so many mixed feelings in me, and I can feel that familiar flutter of panic rise in my chest recalling the memory ... but I have to remind myself that I am safe, and it's important I tell you what happened, as I made a promise to be fully open and honest with you – it's the only way you can empathise and understand.

I was standing in the bustling corridors of Studio 5 at ITV, a place I loved (and fortunately still do), our show shared the studio with *GMTV* and *Lorraine* (which is now home to ITV's *Good Morning Britain*) and we would wait for the live show to come off air, and then our set and team would 'move in' like whirling dervishes for a major overhaul so we could start shooting *Toonattik* an hour later. Studio days were always the most exciting and my favourite, but over the past weeks, due to these horrible unexplained feelings of anxiety, I'd begun to fear the pressures and exposure of it all.

This particular day, back in 2006, I'd never felt so ill, spaced out and downright petrified. I hadn't slept for days ... and instead I'd been lying night after night in bed in the grips of the most horrible thoughts and fear. The night before this particular day, I'd actually been staying at my folks as I was now unable to even cope living by myself in my beloved London flat, and I'd spent the whole night curled up in bed with my mum while she tried to reassure me that I was safe. Here I was, a veteran Children's TV presenter of a number 1 rating show, and yet I was curled up in bed like a toddler with 'mummy', how sad and pathetic do you think I felt?! The answer – excruciatingly so.

I remember just standing in the corridor by the Green Room, Lorraine Kelly had just gone on air which signalled the start of my makeup slot, and I was aware of the hustle and bustle going on around me ... runners making tea, props guys lugging heavy sets about, the GMTV presenters de-mic'ing and breathing a sigh of relief after a morning's work well done. There was one lovely person, who I won't name for fear of embarrassing her, who for some reason thought she should ask how I was, as I was clearly looking anything other than 'well'. It was this one, simple act of kindness and concern that opened the flood gates of no return and I gratefully and pathetically broke down in tears and uttered that so very difficult word: *'Help'*.

To be fair, from that moment on, everyone was great. I had finally acknowledged to myself that I needed help, and crucially, I'd asked for it. My co-presenter Jamie was brilliant, and I shall always be grateful to him for his kindness and action, as he took control of the situation that ensued, speaking to our directors and producers, who then in turn arranged for me to go home at once to rest and get whatever help I needed.

One half of an established (and crucial to the show's narrative) presenting duo, leaving a production in the lurch is never going to be a popular or welcomed choice, but the team I worked with really were just great. Accepting, kind and (even though it was perhaps too little too late as the signs had been brewing for months) fully supportive of me and the choices I needed to make. *Toonattik* remains un-topped as my most favourite career moment so far, and the wonderful team I worked with will always be friends for life.

Fortunately, after this very public meltdown at work, I got the help I so desperately needed, yet until that point, didn't know existed. I WISH someone had shoved this book in my hand, I really do, it would genuinely have helped me feel like a) I wasn't alone and b) that I was normal.

So now on to some semi-technical snazzy stuff ... what actually IS a panic attack and why did I have one?

The 'science-y' bit

For me, the easiest way to think about a panic attack (now), is to regard it as a friend. You're no doubt thinking I've lost the plot, but yes, a panic attack is actually your body's natural defence mechanism to protect you in times of danger or threat, as I explained a little more with how stress affects us in Chapter 1.

So, just to delve a little further and to allow you to start to see the relationship between, stress, anxiety and panic attacks, let me recap.

Back in the day, way back when the cavemen (and woman of course) I was talking about in the last chapter were roaming the land, life was primitive to say the least, with predators at every turn. Hunting was the 'career' of its day, with danger and threat to one's safety at every turn – I'm not sure how calm I'd have felt if a sabre-tooth tiger jumped out at me either! So, a physical response to this state of alert and self-protection manifested itself as a way of ensuring our survival, and it had to be responded to at once, otherwise it'd be dinner time for that tiger. As you now know, this is now widely known in as the Fight, Flight or Freeze response – either you fought the danger, hid from it or you got the hell outta there.

So, do you remember all those symptoms I explained when our caveman ancestor was poised for conflict, with threat to his safety at every turn? Tense muscles ready for action, blood pressure rising and the heart beating faster to increase the blood flow to the muscles in preparation of any extra demands about to be placed on them. His breathing would be getting faster and more shallow to help oxygen get to the blood quicker, making him feel dizzy or lightheaded and perhaps tight chested and in pain. His mouth might become dry and there might be a sudden need to pee (or worse, a number two) as his body halts digestion for a moment, and instead directs as much blood as it can to his 'poised for action' limbs. As a result he may feel queasy, and his body sweats as it tries to cool him down. This is essentially a shedload of adrenalin flooding the body, and as we now know, is commonly known as 'stress hormones'. Aha, all starting to make sense now?

Do any of those feelings sound familiar to you perhaps? Well, much like the anxiety and stress responses in Chapter 1, *that* is precisely what a panic attack is, and can feel like. That is why anxiety is so inextricably linked to panic attacks, stress, and all the other chapters in this book, and it's important for me to highlight it not once, but twice, as it's key to understanding the physical crap we can go through, essentially so we can change the triggers.

Thankfully, nowadays, we don't have massive savage animals or spear-wielding enemies lurking at every turn. But our sophisticated human species has evolved with this core survival skill still built in. Pretty cool on one hand, but extremely irritating and unhelpful when it presents ▶

Activity alert

How to kick a panic attack to the curb!

☺ OK, so you're feeling those familiar sensations ... a pick 'n' mix of the following:

- shallow breathing
- feeling sick
- dizziness
- chest stabbing pains or a grip-like feeling over your heart,
- a cold fear sensation flooding your body
- face getting hot and flushed
- sweaty tingling hands
- a need to use the toilet
- the urge to run away from wherever you are
- feeling in a 'fog'
- scared and freaked out
- tearful
- like you're having a heart attack or dying.

Firstly don't fight the feelings. Don't resist – the quickest way for a panic attack to go away is to let it do its thing ... you know those feelings that are taking hold? That's just the 'survival mode' stress reaction having an outing, giving you a signal that it's in 'alert' mode. ☺ If and when possible, get yourself to a 'safe zone' where you can just 'be' for a few moments in private – maybe the bathroom, a corridor, a quiet corner, and challenge your panic attack to 'come on then – do your worst!' ☺ Allow any feelings to peak (they won't stay there long), and then allow the feelings to wash over you like a cool calming wave, and notice how they dissolve out and away from your body. ☺ Stay in the present. Notice where you are, your surroundings, focus on the hardness of the chair or floor, what you can hear i.e. the traffic outside, the flushing of loos around you, other people talking – and remind yourself of how safe you are. Notice what's really happening to you, not what you think 'might' happen ☺ Let's get some breathing sorted too. First, sit down if you can, or stand up, nice and upright, but in a physically relaxed way. Release

▶

any hunched shoulders, shake out your hands, arms and fingers to relieve any tension, and gently stretch your neck and head from side to side to loosen it up. ☉ **Close your eyes and focus on your breathing. How it feels and sounds. Breathe in for 7 seconds through your nose, pause for a second, and then breathe out again through your mouth for 11 seconds. Repeat this exercise 5 times (it brings more oxygen to the blood and slows down your heart rate).** ☉ You might find at first that you only get as far as a few seconds, but that's totally ok, notice each time you complete a 'set' how far you get and what adjustments need to be made to your technique in order to reach the full target. ☉ **As you start to feel the sensations ebb away, congratulate and reassure yourself that you are absolutely fine. You may feel temporarily fluffy brained, not able to concentrate, think or remember, but don't worry, that will improve too.** ☉ It can be helpful to have an SOS 'phone a friend' on standby. This can be someone you trust to help you through a moment of panic, and be on the end of a phone call or text to guide you through and 'hold your hand' as the feelings ease off. You can even 'train' them to talk you through the breathing steps and do it with you. ☉ **Grab yourself a glass of water, rehydrate that parched palate, and if you'd like to, tell a trusted friend, colleague or family member for some well-earned support and TLC.** ☉ Finally – give yourself a HIGH FIVE! Well done, you got through it, you're still here to tell the tale, and you've successfully given two fingers to a panic attack.

itself as a whopping panic attack in the cheese aisle in Tesco (this actually happened to a client of mine...)

When we understand something, we are far better placed to do something about it and be more in control of it. Fact. And I'm hopeful that you're starting to master this already.

A few more facts and figures

There are lots of conflicting facts, figures and stats out there when it comes to panic attacks. But it's generally accepted that with 1 in 4 of us experiencing a mental health problem at some stage in our lives, the chances of having a panic attack are pretty high. Some experts say everyone will have one at some stage of their life, other reports suggest it's 1 in 10 of us.

Well, whatever the surveys and reports say, it's safe to suggest that anyone can have a panic attack at any time, for any reason. There doesn't have to be a reason – that's the point. Anxiety doesn't discriminate: it can affect anybody regardless of race, religion, gender or background. Mental health and all aspects of it are 'normal'.

If we're going to tackle this stigma and the taboo that surrounds anxiety and mental health, we need to start talking about it in a more relaxed and understandable way for everyone. It's nothing to be ashamed of after all, and we've just established that we're all programmed with the same panic attack system from birth.

Learning to understand what is going on for you, where aspects of your life might benefit from a bit of a 'step back', reducing any stress in your life (see Chapter 8), re-organisation and/or exploration, can really go a long way in making any changes or tweaks to identifying why a panic attack might happen, and ultimately to eliminate that stress trigger to kick it to the curb for good. You can do it! Congratulations, with these anxiety-busting skills, you're well on your way to giving panic attacks a run for their money.

Activity alert

Taking time out

Ideally you should be in a quiet comfortable place, however, you can do this even in a busy office (I have, many times). You just need to allow your mind to shut off for a few minutes and just let the background noise 'be'. ☉ Get yourself into a comfortable position, i.e. sitting cross legged on the floor, curled up on the sofa, sitting on the loo, lying down, at your work station ... you get the gist. ☉ Give yourself permission to absorb yourself in your own thoughts for a few minutes uninterrupted (top tip – if you are in a busy place try wearing headphones so you are less likely to get interrupted), and start to focus on breathing slowly, and deeply, ensuring that on each breath you take and exhale, all tension from your body eases off and flows away out of you. ☉ Take a good few breaths, slowly in for 7 seconds, right down into your tummy making sure it expands, and then breathe out slowly for 11 seconds through your mouth noticing how the air in your tummy gets gradually squeezed out, leaving it empty and ready to be refilled each time. ☉ As you breathe, notice all feelings of tension in your body release, any tight areas or sensations, let them just turn to fluff or warm water, and imagine any 'gripping' feelings just loosening off as though a tight belt has pinged off, letting the sensations float away into nothing. ☉ Well done, you're doing great. Keep the nice controlled breathing going, and as you sit or stand or lie in the moment, close your eyes, and have a think about a time when you've felt calm. If you can't recall a memory, imagine what it might be like to feel calm. ☉ Run this memory or thought over in your mind, enjoying how it feels and noticing what is happening. What can you see? Can you hear anything? Do you have any feelings or sensations in your body? Can you smell or taste anything? ☉ Once you've run the 'scene' over in your mind a few times, make every aspect of it 'better'. Turn any good noise 'up', make the colours brighter, any smells or tastes, imagine them as delicious as can be, and any good feelings you have, make them as rich and concentrated as they can be. ☉ When you are totally absorbed in this wonderful calm moment, make a fist and squeeze as hard as you can for a few seconds, totally letting the heightened sensations take over. ☉ Now, bring yourself back into the present. Well done. How do you feel? A bit calmer? If the answer is 'yes', excellent stuff. If you're not sure, don't worry at all, just try it again, repeating

▶

the same steps until you can transport yourself and feel those 'calm' feelings as intensely as possible. It can take a few goes so have a play, and the more you practise this exercise, the quicker and better it works. ☺ Voila. Your very own 'time out' activity for when you feel those first signs of panic start.

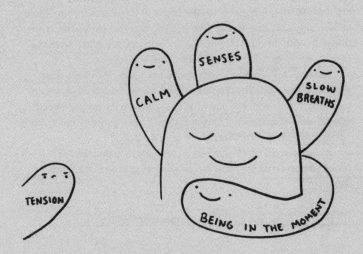

Dr Reetta says...
Panic attacks

I f you have been given the diagnosis of a 'panic disorder', like Anna was, or a mental health professional has assessed you to be experiencing panic attacks, it can feel very scary. I would advise you to visit your GP to rule out any medical issues or physical illnesses, before addressing your panic attacks. The good news is that panic attacks are treatable. With the right information and support, you could overcome them in a couple of sessions of CBT or similar therapy.

Talking back to your thoughts can make a huge difference when anxious, including during panic attacks. Let's say you could wipe away the thought 'My heart is racing and I'm breathless, I'm having a heart attack!' and replace it with, 'This is anxiety, I can tolerate it, it will pass in a few moments.' What difference would this make?

Anna's activity of 'How to kick a panic attack to the curb!' is full of practical strategies that can be adapted to fit almost anyone's situation.

Top tips for tackling panic attacks

Top tip 1
During a panic attack, it can sometimes feel almost impossible to think clearly or remember whatever you planned to do when you were calmer.

How about writing down the strategies that are most 'you'? And carrying these with you, whether it's on your phone or a piece of paper in your bag? Some of my clients have designed a credit card-sized note with the most useful strategies and coping statements ('I've been through this before and nothing bad has happened', 'keep breathing calmly, it will help', or 'I can accept this situation, I know it will pass'). So next time you are panicking and perhaps hiding in the toilet cubicle, reach for your notes to help you get through the panic.

▶

Top tip 2

Expose yourself to the situations that you fear. Make a list of these situations and, starting with the easiest, gradually desensitise yourself. Get used to the awful feelings of panic. When you are in the situation (and remember Anna's advice about breathing), stay with the fear and don't leave it until your anxiety has come down.

Top tip 3

Use distraction and focus on the world around you through your senses. Instead of focusing on yourself and how awful you feel, do what Anna suggested in 'stay in the present' in the 'How to kick a panic attack to the curb' section.

3
SOCIAL ANXIETY – THE '*GET ME OUT OF HERE NOW!*' FEELING

GET ME OUT OF HERE!

Anna's Quick Fix SOS

HAVE AN EXIT PLAN There's nothing worse than feeling 'trapped' in a situation. Calm yourself with the knowledge that you can leave at any time you like. You are in control.

FOCUS ON OTHERS By diverting the attention from you to others can be a quick effective way to shift the anxious, self-conscious feelings. Ask questions and allow yourself to just 'be' in a situation until you feel more comfortable.

FAKE IT, FEEL IT! Trick yourself into how you 'want' to feel. Have a play by being the best actor in the world and adopt the poise of a confident relaxed person. Once you fake it, you can actually 'feel' it.

#Awkward!

Social anxiety is a term that is bandied around a lot nowadays. I reckon that most people, at one time or another feel those awkward insecure feelings when it comes to a social scene or event. Let's have a think about it for a moment, we're surrounded by situations which require us to get suited and booted, dust off our sparkling wit and conversational skills, and throw us into a social free for all. It could be a family wedding, a work presentation, a birthday party or an office drinks night – the situations we can find ourselves in can be really challenging, even for the sociable butterflies among us.

Trust me, I know. People for years have always remarked that I must be the most confident person in the world – with a career on the telly I guess could give off that impression, it's a fair observation, but it might surprise you to know that I started out my life as the most painfully shy child you could ever meet.

One of my most vivid memories was accompanying my mum to the butchers on her shopping rounds, I was so terrified of anyone talking to me that I hid my face the vast majority of the time in my mum's long 80s skirts. I remember this particular time that the friendly butcher leaned over his counter to loudly remark 'ello darlin' what ya hiding for?!' ... as nice a chap as I'm sure he was, my response at having this portly chap bark in my face was sheer fear and a prompt burst into tears.

I was so shy that I would hide from my cousins for hours when they came to visit, and when I started primary school I was so terrified of having to mix with other kids and make friends that I refused to go out to play at break-time and spent months on my tod in the school library until a kindly girl called Lauren, heavily prompted by the teacher, took pity and befriended me.

It took careful nurturing and understanding from the teachers and others kids, but in no time at all, I went from a terrified self-imposed isolated child, to gradually build up my confidence, and most importantly for others to have confidence in me, and in only a year or two, I ended up becoming the school head of house – I still have the chipped green badge as proof of my achievement and it's truly one of my most treasured possessions – it signifies so much.

Nowadays, on the whole, I'm a fairly confident person in social situations, but there are still times where I totally brick myself and feel the heat from the familiar anxiety pangs threatening to blow my cool calm exterior. As a presenter, I'm often popping to a red carpet showbiz do, and not once do I ever turn up feeling anything but nervous, awkward and socially inept – even if just for a short time. There's the pressure of, 'who's there?', 'what if I lose my ticket?', 'what if no one will talk to me?', 'what if the photographers ask for my picture?', 'eek, what if the photographers DON'T ask for my picture!?' ... the endless niggling fears reverberate about my person like a pinball machine on a sugar rush.

And then take a family do or work party. There can be such an expectation to 'be' a certain way and to live up to expectations in all kinds of ways, what we look like, how we stand and hold ourselves, what we say, what we ask ... the elements of socially interacting are endless, and I don't believe *anyone* breezes it all the time.

What *is* social anxiety?

So, what actually is it and why do so many people suffer from it? So many people report feelings of anxiety in social settings, it's increasingly common and you're certainly not alone. In fact, I'd put money on it that more people feel like a prize wally in a social setting than those who don't, so perhaps food for thought next time you're out and about, take solace and comfort in the fact that we are in fact *all* quietly papping our pants.

Social anxiety is a specific form of anxiety, it's an emotion characterised by a discomfort or a fear when a person is in a social interaction that involves a concern of being judged or evaluated by others. It is typically characterised by an intense fear of what others are thinking about them (specifically fear of embarrassment or humiliation, criticism or rejection), which results in the individual feeling insecure and not good enough for other people, and/or the assumption that peers will automatically reject or judge them. Paranoia is often felt by sufferers, and it's altogether a pretty un-fun situation and thought process to be in.

People vary in how often they experience social anxiety and in which kind of situations can trigger it. Everyone is wonderfully different and there isn't one size fits all. However, there are some more common symptoms and situations that you may have some experience with, or at the very least, some empathy with.

Most common social anxiety triggers

So many situations can cause us to shrivel up and cower quicker than the timid Lion in the *Wizard of Oz*, I remember school was the biggest hurdle for me from day one. My earliest memory was being physically removed from my mother on my first day of nursery school, I was *not* up for playing with a bunch of new kids, I was quite happy hanging out with my Ma thank you very much. Fortunately I soon settled in, and my poor Mum got over feeling like the worst parent in the world as I quickly got used to the new scene I was expected to thrive and socialise in, but given the choice, I very much believe my four-year-old self would have further resisted to come out of my comfort zone if I could have got away with it.

Of course, this isn't feasible in everyday life, if we didn't get out, socialise and interact with others it would seriously hinder our social and communication skills. Mixing with others in a range of different settings is helpful to our development, regardless of our age, and the more we do it, hopefully the more used to it we become.

As you know from me by now, I used to hate coming out of my comfort bubble, but I'm jolly glad that over my formative years I learnt the benefits from socialising with others and my communication skills gradually improved, and the more they became second nature, the easier I found it to mix with others. I believe there is no rocket science to it, a lot of it is belt and braces, head up, plaster a smile on the face and give it a good go. Easier said than done for sure, but there are some cunning little tips and techniques to help you cope in whatever social situation you find yourself.

The most common situations that people report feeling particularly socially anxious in include:

- Family functions and get-togethers
- Work parties and events
- Weddings and christenings
- Friend reunions
- Going to a pub or club alone
- Eating out in a restaurant
- Presentations and/or speeches
- Random celebrations i.e. birthdays, exam results, etc.

I'm sure you could add a few others of your own choice to this list too. There seems to be a common theme with a lot of these situations of

potential anxiety, and that is ... it's the unknown. Not knowing what is going to happen, who is going to be there, and what the outcome of the day/evening will be can be the perfect trigger of a massive bout of social anxiety. When you think about it, it makes perfect sense doesn't it ... who *wouldn't* be nervous about something that hasn't happened yet?! There are so many variables, right? This is where we can start to arm ourselves with a few cheeky and handy techniques to get ourselves into a more resourceful and empowered state from the get go. ▶

Activity alert

Weighing it up

Getting yourself in a fully clued up and knowledgeable state is a great way to start your social activity of choice. If you have the luxury of time and reflection, before you even make your mind up, or decide on attending said event, ask yourself these questions, and most importantly notice the answers:

What WILL happen if I DO go to...? ☺ What WILL happen if I DON'T go to...? ☺ What WON'T happen if I DO go to...? ☺ What WON'T happen if I DON'T go to...?

This series of questions can be a hugely helpful tool in helping ascertain how you feel about what you're about to experience, and can help you weigh up the situation to get the best outcome for you.

Give them a go, write down the answers if you like so you have a record of them, and allow the clarity to empower you to have a good understanding of what you're about to do and why.

Let's get physical

Anxiety in general comes attached to some rather funky, and at times annoyingly unpleasant and embarrassing physical symptoms, and social anxiety is the perfect showcase for some of the more obvious ones.

Sweating, needing the loo, excessive flatulence, blushing, muscle tension, all are signs that someone is not quite feeling the most relaxed. Take a moment now, if you can, to notice how you react in a typical social situation, maybe some of the symptoms I've just mentioned resonate with you, and maybe you've got some of your own unique traits to add too.

I recently went to a work 'do' in London by myself, which I'm quite used to doing. I can't say I love turning up to something by myself, particularly if I don't know anyone there and what to expect, but sometimes my work depends on swanning around showing my face at events, regardless of whether I've managed to rope someone in to come along with me or not.

This particular event was one of those snobby cliquey functions, held in a swanky hotel with fizz, canapés and people on the doors with clipboards. Having rather mastered the art by now after years of socialising, I boldly strutted into the function room ready to embrace whatever was coming. Well, that aforementioned bravado disappeared in a puff of smoke as I was met with a wall of 'rubber necking' po-faces, all clambering to see who was arriving next, and I was shocked to discover my usual cool calm exterior was suddenly wracked with anxiety and insecurity. Cue the shrinking body language, pumping heart, the dry mouth and sudden dart for the champagne tray to give me something to do (and down for Dutch courage!), and as I stood awkwardly in a corner of the room I pulled out my comfort 'crutch' – my mobile phone – to try and look vaguely occupied and less like the total Billy no mates, saddo that I clearly felt, and must have looked.

Pretending to be on some important work email, and yet actually scouring Kim Kardashian's latest trivial Instagram post, I attempted to style it out for all of five minutes before admitting defeat, grabbing my ▶

coat, and letting the anxiety win as I scuttled out of the party, tail between my legs.

I was so frustrated with myself – why did I let the situation take hold of me like that? What was it that made me feel so anxious and insecure? What could I have done to conquer and face that fear? The answer – I hadn't prepared myself for what I was going into. My lack of 'pre-show planning' had left my fears and insecurities wide open to be judged and gawped at. The next exercise is a great reminder to me, and one of my personal favourite tools which is used widely in coaching, and it's a handy technique you might like to give a try too should you find yourself in a similar situation.

What's the worst that can happen?

Often having this little saying in the forefront of your mind can be a huge help in getting some instant control and perspective on a situation. I have some clients who come to me so wound up, full of fear, presenting several symptoms, and yet when we unpick what the impending social anxiety actually is, it's amazing how we find little evidence to back up such an extreme reaction. Often the *thought* of what we're about to do is so much worse than the actual event, how mad is that? And how unfair are we being to our poor nerves and confidence.

Evidence is a huge factor. I love working with evidence, as it's our own personal guide to gaining clarity and perspective on a situation quick smart. When I have a client, or friend – or even myself when I need a good talking to – who is experiencing anxiety at a social situation, I very quickly move them to exploring what evidence they have that tells them this anxiety is justified. It may or may not surprise you to know that most people fall short of coming up with anything decent to reason their fears – in fact, most people suddenly look a tad confused and unsure about what on earth they're worried about in the first place. Confusion in this instance is good: it means we're questioning our reactions.

I had a client who suffered with a real phobia of socialising in large groups of new people such as a work meeting, or a drinks party. ▶

Activity alert

Plan it out ... play it out

Having a plan, in pretty much everything we do in life, is a great asset to have. It serves as a handy reminder of what's coming up, what we want to do and how we're going to achieve what we've set out to do. It also limits unwelcome surprises so helps to keep that control and grounding that is so important when taking charge of anxiety.

Take a piece of paper, your smartphone 'notes', or whatever you'd like to write this down – it's important that you *do* write it down as we can then be held accountable to our own choices. This is your own GROW model so fill in each 'letter' with your own answers based on the suggested questions.

⊖ *G* is for GOAL
What is it you want to achieve with your social situation?
Where do you want to be and how do you want to feel?
Write down in a positive statement or sentence what your goal is, i.e. 'I will enjoy this event and be proud of myself'

⊖ *R* is for REALITY
Let's get some perspective ... what is your situation now?
Jot down any fears or reservations you may have, and feel free to be as honest with yourself as possible
How are you feeling with regards to the goal?

⊖ *O* is for OPTIONS
This is the exciting empowering bit ... get creative and write down ideas of what you're going to do when you are in your social situation
What strengths do you have that will see you through to your goal?
What resources do you have, people you know, things that have worked before that will help you?
What else can you think of to help you reach the goal?

⊖ *W* is for WILL (motivation)
Time to get empowered and realise how fab and strong you are

▶

How much do you want to achieve this goal?
What will it mean to you?
What will it give you if you achieve your goal?
How much do you deserve it?

Take yourself through these steps for every scenario you might need a bit of a helping hand. By creating your own GROW model, it can really help give some much-needed clarity, strength and focus to getting through a tough situation. You've SO got this.

Every time he had to interact with others he would have such an intense fear of blushing in front of people, thus causing himself such a degree of embarrassment and self-awareness that it nigh on ruined his life. The more he worried about it happening and what others would think of him, the more he withdrew from going out and avoided work engagements, preferring to slope into a corner unnoticed.

When we explored this very real fear and feeling, through his own self-exploratory exercise, he realised that he'd actually only ever blushed in public once, and even then, no one, NOT ONE person had actually made a comment or openly noticed. The feeling he felt was so intense and personal that it clouded his own judgement of what others saw and how that in turn made him feel.

Once he had reasoned with his feelings, his fears and taken note of the evidence, which suggested that he had actually never been ridiculed or judged or made fun of for blushing, guess what happened? The power of the fear was suddenly dramatically reduced. With his tried-and-tested evidence, with a new sense of perspective my client tested out his newfound clarity at a social function, and guess what? The blushing never arose. Bingo! It's been 3 years now and sometimes he may get embarrassed, but as we've explored and reasoned, that's a perfectly ok and normal reaction to have to certain situations, but his intense fear of blushing which caused such a degree of social anxiety has now all but disappeared and he's able to go wherever, whenever and with whoever he chooses.

So, what's the lesson to be learned here? We can be so hard on ourselves and allow the 'fear of the fear' to creep in and take over when we really shouldn't. By keeping a good healthy grip on what the situation and feelings attached to it actually are, we have the best chance of batting off any pesky niggles that threaten any social anxiety to take over and spoil things.

Other helpful tips and if all else fails

As I've demonstrated so far, it can be useful to always have a little think about what situation you're about to be faced with. It's important ▶

Activity alert

Borrow a buddy

This is a great exercise for even the most shy and retiring among us. It's also rather a fun way to discover the inner actor in you. The premise of this is 'fake it, feel it, be it', and it really works.

Have a think about someone you admire and like how they conduct themselves in a social setting. Perhaps it's someone you know, or it could even be a favourite celebrity. ⊙ Take a moment to think about, and visualise them. Notice all aspects of how they behave, hold themselves, their body language, and allow yourself to get a really good understanding of them using all your senses – what they sound like, look like, feel like. It might be helpful to even look at video clips or social media posts to help you make the vision as strong as possible. ⊙ With this person in mind, what you're going to do is 'borrow' some of the traits you most admire, particularly when it comes to socialising. ⊙ Have a think about how they might be feeling, what thoughts might go through their mind when they're in a social setting, and what they might do to prepare themselves. ⊙ It's all in the 'pre show' prep (as I like to call it). Before you take part in your social interaction of choice, allow yourself a quiet moment to absorb yourself in the traits of your chosen 'buddy', really notice the confident thoughts, their body and eye language, how they walk and stand, and what they do that makes you think they're totally at one with themselves in that environment. ⊙ It's show time. Armed with this set of borrowed skills, allow yourself to 'play' at being this person whilst going about your social event. Notice how much easier it feels to put the responsibility in your 'buddy' and just enjoy going through the motions you've already rehearsed mentally, and if you wish, physically, in private. ⊙ Keep tweaking and building on this set of borrowed skills, maybe you could even incorporate someone else's whose traits you want to emulate to make the experience stronger and more confident still. ⊙ In time, once this tried and tested method has built up your own evidence and self-confidence that you CAN socialise and get through it more easily, you can then allow the 'buddy borrowing' traits to ease off as you trust in your own superbly honed socialising skills.

Pat on the back – mentally thank your 'buddy' and well done!

not to overthink it as that can be counterproductive, but by being as prepared and clued up as we can be, it can help eliminate any unhelpful anxiety that may creep up on us at the last minute.

A good skill to develop is to have some small talk prepared, some questions and a few interesting facts about yourself that you tuck away in your conversation bank, should they be needed to fill some awkward dead air. We've all been there: at a function and you're suddenly faced with a scary boss and your mind goes blank, or being stuck with that person who has the conversation skills of a potato... We can safeguard against being the one standing there gawping like a goldfish with nothing to say.

It's one of the most common side-effects of social anxiety, having a dry mouth and a brain that just suddenly seems to empty of any content whatsoever – it can feel debilitating, embarrassing and only serves to intensify and compound the anxiety further.

So have a think about the Top Three conversation starters you can have as a safety net, in the back of mind or on the tip of your tongue. Avoid 'closed questions' which require a simple 'yes or no' answer and leave you with little time to think of something else to say, and also just stop the chat dead. Instead, think of sentences that automatically require the recipient to answer in detail, what we call an 'open question'. It's a great technique to practise and master. These open questions might give you a bit of a head start or inspiration to come up with your own:

- **'Tell me about'** ... your day/your journey/your family, etc.
- **'What are your thoughts on'** ... the weather/work/politics/the news, etc.
- **'Could you explain a little more about'** ... that project/what you mean by that, etc.
- **'How did you achieve'** ... that work goal/your work–life balance/ your wedding budget etc.

You see how by phrasing questions and conversations in this way, it makes it very difficult for the person you're interacting with to give you short one-worded answers, which could otherwise leave you feeling awkward and nervous. This way, the outcome is much more likely to create a proper conversation and one you can then embrace and get stuck in to, thus dissolving any anxiety that might be floating around.

Finally

You've hopefully gained a better understanding and some positive ideas of how to tackle social anxiety from reading this chapter. But if you've tried all the tips and techniques and for some reason on a particular day you just can't shift the niggles of a social anxiety bout, then fear not ... have an exit plan.

Ideally it's better to tackle the nerves and anxiety head on as we've explored, but if it really does get too much, don't worry at all about having a cunning 'get me out now' exit plan. I've used it myself from time to time, and it's totally ok to do so and important to remember that we're never trapped anywhere as long as we have the will, motivation and mobility to move.

If you're in a meeting or a crowded pub, have a scope of where the doors and available exits are, and plan where you might sit or stand to allow you easier access to them should you need to duck out at a moment's notice. Have a think too about being as open and honest as you feel comfortable doing so with friends and colleagues about how you're feeling. Often, by starting a dreaded speech or presentation, or conversation to a stranger, it can be a great caveat and lighten the mood (mainly yours!) to actually say *'I'm feeling rather nervous so do bear with me'*, or telling your mate that you're feeling a tad anxious, you'll find most people are empathic and sympathetic. Remember what I said at the beginning of the chapter, so many people experience social anxiety so chances are they'll totally get what you mean and be kind to your situation.

By setting these plans in motion, more often than not takes most of the anxiety away instantly, and you'll probably find you'll never actually need to make use of your carefully planned escape route – knowing it is there can be comfort and security enough.

Have fun playing with these tools and techniques, and enjoy the empowerment I hope you get from knowing that a) you're not alone and b) social anxiety ... pah, WHAT social anxiety?

Dr Reetta says...
Social anxiety

As Anna says, social anxiety is very common. People who suffer from it have negative thoughts about themselves and think that things will go badly in social situations. People often know that their fears are irrational, but the problem still persists. Do remember that your thoughts aren't actual facts. Is it fair or helpful to make those guesses about how you'll do in a situation? Let's have a think, could you say something more helpful or realistic to yourself when you are next in a situation that you fear? For example, 'I don't need to be perfect to be liked', 'It's ok to feel anxious, this makes me human'. Nothing will instantly get rid of your social anxiety, but with the strategies Anna described in her 'activity alerts' and challenging your thoughts can help dial it down.

What is your worst fear about social situations? With my clients it is often around others not liking them, thinking they are stupid or boring, or noticing their physical symptoms (blushing, sweating, shaking, etc.). When you feel anxious about a social situation, you will become very self-focused and start self-monitoring as well as paying excessive attention to signs of 'danger'.

People often perform 'safety behaviours', which provide temporary relief, but can lead to them seeming more awkward or even less likable. Anna described a social event where she used her mobile phone as a comfort 'crutch', a classic 'safety behaviour' which I think most of us do to some extent these days. This probably reduced her anxiety in the moment, but long-term will keep her anxiety going about this non-threatening situation. Some other common safety behaviours are: talking quickly, avoiding attracting attention, pretending you didn't see someone, or laughing to hide your nervousness.

Top tips for tackling social anxiety

Top tip 1
To tackle your individual 'safety behaviours', which are preventing you from learning from anxiety-provoking situations, I am going to ask

▶

you to work towards 'exposure': In other words, to face your fears. Your anxiety is telling you to play it safe and do whatever you are used to doing, which keeps your belief about the situation as dangerous going. To overcome your social anxiety, I challenge you to challenge yourself, and do the opposite to what you are used to doing. So if you normally try to avoid any attention, do something to attract attention! If you normally pretend you didn't see someone, go to them and ask how they are. You get the idea. Doing the opposite to what you normally do will allow your body to learn that there is nothing to fear, and your mind to learn that you have the skills to cope.

Top tip 2
Could you say something more helpful or realistic to yourself when you are next in a situation that you fear? For example, 'I don't need to be perfect to be liked', 'It's ok to feel anxious, this makes me human'.

Top tip 3
Finally, have a think about the spectrum of 'normal' in social situations. If you think of a group of people in a social occasion, how many 'acceptable' or 'normal' ways of behaving are there? Next time you attend a social gathering, observe the people around you and you will probably notice that many display possible anxious behaviours. Anxiety is part of our world, the same way happiness, sadness, and anger are. If your anxiety shows in social situations, this may even have some positive outcomes associated with it, for example, you may seem more approachable, or you may be thought of as being modest which by many is seen as attractive.

4

INSOMNIA – THE *'TICK TOCK WON'T STOP'* FEELING

Anna's Quick Fix SOS

DE-STRESS! Going to bed all burdened and with pent-up feelings from the day isn't going to help evoke sleep. Notice any feelings of stress, and work through ways to ease them off and out.

GET UP Don't lie in bed staring at the ceiling, clock watching all night. Quietly get up, get a herbal tea and read a chapter of a calming book to stimulate sleep.

TALK IT OUT Identify someone trusted you could call and/or talk to for a quick reassuring chat to remind you that you're not alone.

Time for bed (argh!)

When I was at the height of my anxiety, night-time was one of the worst times of day for me. I used to dread it. From the moment I 'woke' – I say 'woke' as it was a fractious rollercoaster of a night to navigate – I feared the next night looming ... like a countdown to Doomsday. When one is highly emotionally and mentally stressed, sleep isn't going to be a walk in the park. When your mind is full of the day that has just been, perhaps full of unresolved worries and issues, and then thoughts of the next day creeping in, our head can feel like it's reached the 'memory full' status of your smartphone, and when it's like that, the last thing that will come easily is sleep. Makes sense right?

Perhaps take a moment to think about your own experiences of sleep. Can you remember a time when you've had a really good snooze (think a Joey and Chandler nap in *Friends*), or an uninterrupted night of being purely zonked out – you know the kind, where you wake up in exactly the same position you fell asleep in 8 hours previously, ahhh it's just heaven. Arguably there is nothing more wonderful and refreshing than a corking night's sleep. It's bliss.

On the flip side, can you recall a time when you've had a terrible time in bed – ahem, and I mean for sleep reasons! Perhaps, like me, you're a fully signed up member of the 'early hours clock-watching' club, your sleep may be frequently interrupted with disturbing dreams, or you might be up more times to the loo in the night than a jack in the box, all these can be signs that your quality of sleep needs to be addressed, and given a hefty dose of TLC. Why is this important? Well, when we're lacking in good-quality sleep, our mental, as well as physical health, can start to suffer and deteriorate, causing all kinds of other associated and unwanted symptoms to crop up, such as depression, OCD (obsessive compulsive disorder), eating issues and anxiety.

My story

Sharing this part of my story is arguably one of the hardest and rawest, because it's the most exposing emotionally for me. As I have done all throughout this book, I've endeavoured to be completely honest and open with you as that's the whole point of you reading this – to get a *real* insight into how it can feel as an anxiety sufferer, not an edited version, and to shine a light on the various interlinked symptoms that can be experienced by any of us, at any time.

During my anxiety and panic attack battle, insomnia and sleep deprivation was one of the most difficult and key parts of my symptoms. When you have little or no sleep, the anxiety, panic, depression, etc. is only going to get worse. With no resources left in the tank and your poor energy stores running increasingly on empty, it stands to reason that the rest of you, mentally, emotionally and physically, would start to struggle and breakdown. It's no coincidence that a form of torture used by captors is to keep a captive awake for several days and sleep deprived, it can drive you mad – literally, and render you a complete and utter shadow of your former self.

Fortunately nothing as dramatic as that here, although anyone that suffers with insomnia will empathise that it *can* feel like torture ... except it's self-imposed, and often feels out of our control, which in a way can feel just as bad.

My panic attacks and anxiety had been brewing for months, a combination of a toxic relationship at home, and a people pleasing nature at work, and with friends and family, had lead me head first into a ticking timebomb of anxiety and depression. I spent so much time and energy making sure I was all things to all people that I left little, if anything, for myself. That, my friends, is not a good recipe for a healthy mental wellbeing. The main problem was though, that I couldn't see it coming. I knew I was feeling rubbish and as though I was treading water each day, just about getting by, but I had no idea that I was increasingly running on empty to the point that if my mind was one of those cartoon dynamite sticks, bound and attached to a runaway train, someone had well and truly lit the fuse and it was rapidly getting to the 'boom'!

So where does sleep come into this? And how is it so linked to my anxiety disorder? Well, after several months of feeling these daily pangs of fear, I found myself working away for a few months on a new telly job. It was hard graft and I frequently had to commute back and forth to London to continue my *Toonattik* filming commitments too. This was all my decision I hasten to add, and perhaps now with the wonderful benefit of hindsight, I should have paced myself MUCH better.

I was staying in a hotel for much of this period, and my on/off boyfriend at the time, who let's just say wasn't the most compatible of partners so it turns out, would sometimes visit. The unease I was feeling in my relationship, added to the already frayed nerves and exhaustion at juggling two jobs, was already taking its toll. The signs were there, but not being any wiser at this stage of my relatively inexperienced life, I didn't know how to spot them or indeed do anything about them.

I'd always prided myself on being a good sleeper, and perhaps took it for granted that I was able to kip anywhere. I was the kind of child who could fall asleep on a gravel driveway, and later in life, enjoy a good powernap in the back of cab, until this point I'd never known what sleep interruption felt like, so I soon began to feel the effects of how a not so perfect sleep feels.

My bedtime routine was beginning to be eaten into with worry. It was a gradual process at first ... I didn't really notice it creep up on me, it just suddenly one day became a major issue which in turn served as my anxiety and panic attack trigger.

It was around this time, living away, that I was one night going to bed, with the hope of a much needed quality sleep as I had work to get up for, and the on/off boyfriend happened to be staying over too. As I've said, it was a tricky situation and I had a lot going on, so I wasn't feeling my most relaxed. This particular night, I'd gone to bed early and alone desperate for some peace and quiet from the world.

I had just dropped off into an uneasy, yet established slumber, when a huge door slam from another room startled me bolt upright in bed. It was no one's fault, but this simple act shot my already knackered nerves once and for all, it was the dynamite 'boom' that had been fizzing along. I woke up fully alert and in 'fight or flight' startled mode, with what I can only describe as the mother of all panic attacks shooting through my entire body like a firework. I didn't know at the time what on earth I was experiencing, but I felt so horrendous and as though I was dying, so I was absolutely petrified. I was alone and in desperate need of someone to comfort and reassure me.

Dazed, terrified and unsure of what the hell was happening to me, I somehow navigated myself and ran out of the building to my parked car, and stood like a rabbit caught in headlights, uncertain of which turn to take. It was 2am, I was in my PJs, it was snowing and I was in a town I didn't know. Somehow I made my way back into the hotel and my room, and as the feelings of panic and fear gradually subsided, I 'settled' in foetal position on a nearby sofa – by this point the boyfriend was back, oblivious and snoring on the bed nearby.

It was at this moment that I realised I needed security and comfort. A reassuring word of kindness and familiarity to tell me I was ok and wasn't going to die alone ... so I called my mum.

Little did I know at the time, but this simple act of calling my darling mother in the early hours begging for reassurance sparked the start of a little 'crutch' that I relied on for several months following – and if I'm totally honest I still do to some extent, although I make sure the hour is a little more civilised.

I'm sure she was worried sick, but as I rang her on this inaugural night, my mum didn't let any of her emotion show as she calmly 'talked me down' and through this massive wallop of a panic attack. Little did I know at the time, but hearing what I was experiencing, my mother had several years earlier also had her fair share of anxiety attacks following a miscarriage, so she identified very quickly what was happening to me – and thank God she did, because I didn't have a clue.

The panic attack had peaked and finally eased off by sunrise and I was able to fall into an exhausted sleep on the couch, yet unbeknown to me, the damage had already been done. What was to follow over the coming months, was the familiarity of 'learned behaviour', and a cycle of fear began to develop each time I was about to go to bed. The panic attack I had experienced while I was in bed was SO awful, isolating and petrifying, that I feared another one happening again. The fear of having a panic attack alone and in bed again had set in, perpetuating more fear, and thus a 'disorder' had been created.

I spend a lot of time with my private clients helping them identify triggers for certain behaviours and symptoms, for there very nearly always is one, and having had one myself, it can make it easier to empathise and delve into where we need to go, in order to dig it out and work on it. That was a big part of my therapy when I eventually sought help, and I've never looked back.

Taking us back to this first and defining panic attack episode in that hotel away from the safety and familiarity of my home, it sparked a series of unhelpful behaviour including the sleep phobia that soon took over my day-to-day routine. I began to get obsessed about going to bed at a certain time and counting how many hours of sleep I got. I would start to feel the anxiety rise in my chest around 6pm each day as I anticipated bedtime approaching, and it steadily got worse and more intense as the minutes ticked by.

By the time it was vaguely time for bed – I'd imposed a 9pm lights-out rule for some reason, to ensure I'd get plenty of kip – I was such a worked up, stressed and anxious mess that the last thing my poor mind and body was capable of doing, was sleep. Added to this I'd just learnt a hefty script for the next day, so my brain was buzzing with words and stage directions, and I was in no fit state to chill and take on the much-needed zzzzs to recharge.

I'd climb into bed, alone (by this point I'd made the decision to be single again), turn the light out ... wait ... and then ... BOOM! The familiar feeling I'd experienced in bed that time once again came out to play ... it crept up from the bottom of my tummy, and then like a wave rushed up into my chest and heart with such force and ferocity it attacked my torso like a red hot poker. I'd lie there, in the dark, terrified. So, what did I do ... yes, I called my mum for those reassuring soothing words that would at least take the edge off.

im tired, I should sleep

can't sleep. I should stay up and worry

perfection

The phone call would help and made me feel less alone, but with so much adrenalin running through my body, I never calmly went to sleep afterwards. I would toss and turn for several hours, watching each hourly milestone come and go, until eventually, presumably exhausted, I'd drop off.

I began to try herbal sleeping pills, then even proper hardcore sleeping tranquilisers – I was desperate for sleep – nothing really worked, and if anything I'd just feel groggy and more exhausted the next day. In essence, having already been suffering and (badly) coping with anxiety pangs for some time, the impact of the panic attack while in bed, and the subsequent no sleep, pretty much tipped me over the edge towards 'meltdown day'. When I see clients now who are clearly stressed at a certain point with their anxiety, I always check in regarding their sleep to find out a) whether they're getting any and b) the quality of it – for that is key too. In my experience, getting a handle on your bedtime and sleep routine can go a long way to helping you keep in control and keeping anxiety at bay.

First up, I want to help you prepare for a good night's sleep.

Good sleep vs bad sleep

You'll have no doubt heard people refer to the fact they've 'had a good sleep'. Equally you may be familiar with the phrase, 'urgh, I've had a terrible night' – it's one of those British pleasantries, along with commenting on the weather, we can really measure our day by how many zzzs we've had the night before.

When you break it down and actually explore what sleep is, it can be interesting, and telling, to notice that the stages and quality of sleep really do correlate to how well we might feel and perform as a result of it.

There are various stages of sleep we dip in and out of. I won't overload you with the full War and Peace version, but in a nutshell we have two phases: Slow Wave sleep, and Dream sleep, also known as REM sleep (Rapid Eye Movement). Both are equally important and occur at different stages of our sleep cycle.

▶

Activity alert

The 3 P's – Plan, Prepare and Peace

Getting ourselves into a good state is key in helping us get the best possible chance to have some decent shut-eye. We can help ourselves by being more self-aware and making some tweaks here and there to give us the best possible chance:

☺ PLAN – don't be confused with having to come up with some mammoth stressful pre-sleep schedule – that would defeat the object of trying to be calm and relax. But DO have a think about what you're going to do with your evening, what jobs and tasks need doing, and that includes anything social, and give yourself a loose idea of what you need to do and, essentially what you don't – what can be left until another day?

> By having a rough plan in place, and being realistic with it, we can ensure we don't take on too much of our evening, and instead make sure we leave crucial wind down time before you go to sleep to help get your mind and body into a relaxed sleepy state.

☺ PREPARE – it's all in the preparation in a lot of things we do in life, and preparing for a good night's sleep is another of our daily activities that benefits from a little bit of insight.

> Once you've planned what you are going to do, prepare *how* you're actually going to go about it. If you have jobs to do, have an idea about when in the day/evening you're going to do them so you can get them completed in good time, way ahead of 'down time'.

> Prepare to come offline, and be uncontactable for the evening, crucially that hour before going to bed. If it helps, tell anyone you need to that you'll be 'out of office', professionally and personally, from a certain time. Don't be tempted to answer that last late-night email or social media post, it can wait until morning – prepare to physically and mentally shut down and allow your mind to slow down, relax and calm. Everyone is entitled to have some quiet time, so be confident in implementing that. You deserve it.

▶

○ PEACE – choose an activity that brings about a sense of peace, quiet and calm. Physically quieting down our body also helps our mind wind down too. Make sure your house is as quiet as possible too.

Perhaps a nice warm bath with candles, a relaxing piece of music or radio station, a favourite fictional book ... choose something which evokes a real sense of peace, and allow yourself to fully shut off from the day-to-day treadmill as you enjoy your downtime.

Once you're ready and feeling suitably relaxed, and hopefully, tired, take yourself off to bed and allow yourself to continue the relaxed feelings until you feel ready to turn in. Night night.

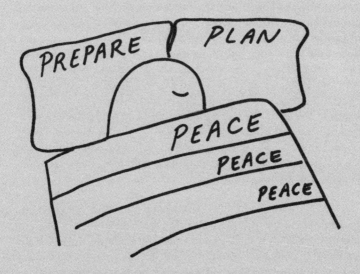

Slow Wave sleep is essential for repairing and restoring the daily wear and tear on some of the 'physical' stuff, our muscles, brain cells and immune system. Dream (REM) sleep is responsible for the emotional TLC our mind and body need each day.

A healthy pattern of sleep for someone to wake up feeling refreshed, relaxed and raring to go for the day ahead usually consists of 90 minutes of Slow Wave sleep, followed by the first 'instalment' of Dream (REM) sleep. As the night evolves, the amount we dip in and out of Dream sleep increases as the Slow Wave sleep eases off. The type of sleep we experience just before we wake is usually Dream, which is why we can often remember the last dream we've just experienced.

So, why and how is this important to anxiety? Well, when we're anxious or have worries, issues, or unresolved conflict on our mind, the amount of that super important, repairing Slow Wave sleep we need is decreased in the early part of our sleep cycle, and the Dream sleep kicks in much sooner, playing out any unresolved and 'aroused' emotions. What we don't 'get rid of' emotionally during our waking hours is reconstructed during the Dream part of our sleep, so, for example, the more worry and stress we build up during the day, then perhaps coupled with a whole new set of worries for the next day ahead, such as: 'will I get to my meeting on time?', 'what if I can't pay the mortgage this month?', 'what if I'm too tired tomorrow' – you can imagine how overloaded that poor part of your sleep cycle is going to get.

The right amount of Dream (REM) sleep is fabulous, and restores and repairs our emotional structure. Too much, however, can leave us feeling completely exhausted and more tired when we wake than we perhaps felt before we even got to bed. If those worries from the night before are still whirring around your mind, added into the mix an exhausting night's sleep where your Dream sleep has been having a right old party, perhaps you've even woken yourself up mid-flow during the night due to the interrupt caused by too much early Dream sleep which has overloaded your brain, it stands to reason that any anxious or depressed feelings are going to be exacerbated.

The longer this goes on, the more you're going to feel the effects of a bad night's sleep. If you're not getting the right quality of sleep in the right order, over time, the wear and tear of running on empty will show as your body and mind is under increasing stress and pressure from all the stress hormones coursing around.

I had a client who would suffer from a routinely terrible night's sleep once a week. Each week the stress, worry and pressure from his job would build up to the point where the 'memory bank' was full, and he would experience a night of vivid dreams, broken sleep and anxiety. When we broke it down and explored what was going on with his thoughts and day-to-day patterns, we noticed that things built up ... and up ... and up ... over a series of days with no self-imposed opportunity or outlet to resolve any irritations or problems, and the outcome was this brilliantly rehearsed interrupted sleep pattern. Over the course of a few weeks, we introduced some of the tips I'm sharing with you in this book, to help him take control of his thoughts, emotions and his sleep routine, allowing himself the time and skills to develop and implement a healthier sleep pattern. It didn't take long at all actually, and I'm pleased to say that, other than the odd blip when he forgets to implement the methods (no one's perfect), he enjoys a fairly constant quality of sleep.

So, what can you do about it? By learning to expel and 'brain dump' as best you can any pent-up feelings, events from the day – that goes for positive as well as negative – and general emotions that may have been triggered, gives us all a good chance to get into a resourceful, ready for bed state where we have the best chance to have some decent shut-eye.

Help! I really can't sleep...

Fear not, there might be times when we just cannot sleep. Maybe the build-up of stressful thoughts are at a point where they might take a little more than just one night of chilling and unwinding, or perhaps you're a new parent and your sleep is constantly interrupted by your little one, rendering you a walking zombie each day (as a new mum-to-be myself,

I'm already on alert for this one!), or perhaps you do shift work and find yourself struggling to adjust your forever tampered with body clock, and sleep is fractious to say the least?

The main thing is to try not to get too worked up and stressed about it. Easier said than done I completely appreciate, but as we know from this chapter already, stress and worry equals anxiety and insomnia, so if we aren't going to gain from having a tizz, best we get this in check asap.

So how can we do something about this? What can we try to help our weary sleep-deprived, stubborn mind, and body drop off to the land of nod? And how do we cope with constant broken sleep, which, due to the yo-yo-ing in and out of sleep, can often feel worse than not sleeping at all.

The first thing is know when to give into it, and when not to. Lying in your bed wide awake tossing and turning hour after hour is up there with trying to complete Candy Crush ... it's wholly frustrating, relentless and only serves to consume your thoughts. If you've been in bed with no sign of sleep even remotely crossing your eyelids for more than an hour – get up. Now, be careful, we don't want to reward the brain by giving it anything nice that might validate getting up – in the same way you wouldn't give a small child a chocolate bar if he decided to get up at horrendous-o'clock – otherwise the signal you're giving to the brain is *'ooh this is great, every time I don't sleep I get something good'*. What this will do is install unresourceful behaviour, and perhaps a pattern of unhelpful thoughts each time you can't sleep, as it will 'look forward' to you getting up.

Choose something really dull and uninspiring, and crucially unstimulating to do. Perhaps it's resetting yourself by going through your bedtime routine again, brushing your teeth, popping to the loo, changing your PJs for a fresh pair and fluffing up your bedding to make it cool and inviting once again. Do this with a low-level light to ensure you don't jolt your brain awake any more than it already is, and keep all movements and actions to a dull monotonous tempo to ensure your body is as calm as possible – if your actions are as sleepy as possible, it does go some way to giving a signal to your brain that it's quiet time.

▶

Activity alert

Breathe it out

Utilising our breathing is a fabulously easy way to quickly relax ourselves. So many of us when we're uptight or anxious find ourselves breathing shallowly and quickly, which is just a major 'no' for keeping your mind and body calm. Using this simple exercise can bring us back on track in any situation throughout the day, but also really useful to do before we try the exercise afterwards too.

Find a quiet place to either sit or lie down for a few minutes, if you have to stand, no problem, that can also work. ☉ Take your attention to your breathing and notice the pattern. ☉ **Keep your attention on each breath and as you notice the rise and fall of your breathing, increase the 'in' breath and then the 'out' breath** – taking the in breath in through your nose and slow and long and deep as you can (right to the pit of your tummy), and then releasing the out breath through your mouth nice and controlled, slow and long, until you have no more air left. ☉ Keep this pattern going until you get into a rhythm, noticing each breath as you take and expel it. As you breathe in, imagine all good things, thoughts and feelings (such as calm, peace and motivation) flow in with the breath and into your whole body. As you breathe out, imagine all the negative niggles (such as any stress, anxiety and worries) going with it, no longer part of you or your body. ☉ **Try this pattern of breathing, and expelling any negative rubbish as you breathe out, for about 5 or 6 breaths. This should leave you feeling more calm, relaxed and focused.**

If you're ready for bed, you can go on to this next exercise.

Activity alert

Play it out in your head in bed

Getting in to a 'resourceful state' when you're about to get in to bed and, even more importantly, when you're in your nest, is key to welcoming in the land of nod. Try this sequence each night, and the more you practise, the more effective the feelings can be.

Make sure your room is a comfortable temperature (not too hot) and that the light is either low or off altogether, if you're ready to fall asleep, then perhaps turn off altogether. ⊙ Get yourself into a comfortable position and allow yourself to lie there, closing your eyes and soaking up any natural noises around you (traffic, the clock, etc.). You may even like to have a low-level radio or music on as a 'comfort' if you don't like complete silence. ⊙ Focus on your breathing and allow yourself to take a lovely deep breath, in through your nose as deeply as you can go, and then out gently through your mouth. This will help relax you even more. ⊙ Now I want you to get creative and use your imagination. Don't worry if you've never really tapped into this part of you before, just go with the flow and see what you come up with – there is no right or wrong. We're going to explore 3 of your senses – visual (eyes), auditory (ears) and kinaesthetic (inner feelings/touch). ⊙ Visualise what your lovely sleep is going to look like. Create in your mind the best picture you can conjure up. Have a think about what the most brilliant sleep looks like ... maybe it's sleeping on a fluffy cloud, or under the stars by a beach, or on a super expensive silky soft king-size bed ... make this image as big and luxurious as you can. Play with the lighting and make it as relaxed as you'd like ... perhaps a soft hue, or dusk setting in. ⊙ Next, add some sounds to that wonderfully relaxing inspiring image. What sounds can you hear that help you feel even more relaxed and sleepy? Maybe you can hear the calling of an owl, or the cosy pitter patter of raindrops, or the gentle lap of the ocean waves ... create and add those calming sounds to the image you're already enjoying. ⊙ And finally, I want to take the focus to inside your body. Have a gentle explore of the feelings that this wonderful scene is bringing about and make them even stronger. Perhaps you're feeling all warm in your chest, or

▶

there's a cool calming 'space' in your head ... notice the feelings, enjoy it, and make it even better and intense. ⏾ As you start to enjoy the thought of sleep in this very real state, in your own time just notice the visualisation you've brilliantly brought about. Allow the pictures, and the sounds, and the feelings to merge and flow together as one big, wonderfully relaxing experience, unique to you. ⏾ As you drift in and around the picture, allow yourself to completely succumb to the scene and all the feelings attached. Enjoy it, embrace it and just let it naturally flow as your body and mind experience a fabulous deep relaxation ... as you gradually fall asleep. Night night.

You could also try getting up and doing something really, *really* boring. Remember, we don't want to fire up and stimulate the brain, so keep all actions as chilled as possible. You might like to tackle something mind-numbingly dull such as a bit of ironing – the more pointless the better, i.e. try ironing some socks or tea towels, or you could re-organise your book shelves, tidy up your stationery drawer, or polish your crockery. The key is to almost punish the brain with a boring task, not reward it with something nice such as a movie, or computer game or gripping book. This way, it will soon get the gist that 'if' you need to get up out of bed to ward off the nagging insomnia, it certainly won't get a treat, it will have a drab task to do which will hopefully soon wear off any wide-awakeness and instead stimulate some well-needed rest.

Be careful not to put the kettle on and have a cuppa (particularly anything caffeinated as this will only serve to wake you further) and the same goes for an alcoholic drink and/or cigarette – all are stimulants and will hinder sleep more. If you do need a drink, stick to something boring such as water or a glass of milk – but be sure to pop to the toilet before you go back to bed.

Be strict with yourself re timings. Agree to get up at a certain time, regardless of how much sleep you may or may not have had. Like a small child, if you stick to a routine, no matter how hard it may feel initially, the body soon responds, gets used to the pattern and what is expected of it, and when, and will (hopefully) welcome the prospect of sleep when it comes about the next night. Training your body and brain to stick to a routine can be super helpful in conquering sleep issues.

If you know you're experiencing hit-and-miss sleep, be sure to plan and prepare your lifestyle accordingly. If you know that going out and getting smashed on a Friday night renders you a mess with a four-day hangover, then be smart and think carefully about your plans and any 'come back' that may happen as a result. No one is suggesting that you can't ever go out and enjoy yourself, far from it – having fun is the best anxiety cure out there –but taking a moment to notice how you're feeling and if you're perhaps needing a few days' chill out at a spa rather than a two-night bender to repair yourself and sleep, then *listen* to what your body is telling you. Banking some much-needed rest can set your week up the way you want it to go, rather than starting a new working week feeling tired, anxious and even more sleep-deprived.

Some of us may experience interrupted sleep through other means, having little ones waking in the night, or a needy family member, or perhaps you or your partner work antisocial shifts, which impact your sleep quality. Tough one, but it's important to not try to be a super hero. Sleep deprivation is rough and you'll find most people have experienced it at some time in their lives, sharing how you're feeling can sometimes help in feeling as though you're not alone with your eye bags and weary limbs.

Getting *some* sleep is usually better than getting no sleep, so have a think about when you might be able to factor in a nap or a meditation half hour to bank up some repair rest. Ask for help from others if you need some peace, quiet and no responsibilities. Perhaps a trusted family member could look after your children for a precious hour, or your partner do the chores while you have a kip instead. Snatch whatever you can during those times of broken sleep, don't be a martyr and remember that you owe it to yourself to be the best you can be before you even start to help anyone else.

If you find it hard to sleep in the day, a good meditation or relaxation recording can make all the difference, and is proven to be as effective as sleep in lots of cases. There are loads of sleep apps, websites and audio books on offer nowadays so enjoy finding something that works for you.

And finally

Hopefully you're feeling a little more clued up about how to give yourself the best chance at a decent night's sleep, and how to help yourself by dealing with any unresolved, pent-up feelings or issues before you hit the sack.

There are a few other bits and bobs we can do as a 'checklist' to ensure we are doing all we can to get into sleep mode, and to give ourselves a fighting chance at some quality serene snoozing.

Do's

Do – make sure you prepare yourself well for sleep, like you would a baby, and have some 'down time' before bed, take a warm bath with some nice smellies, read a good book (nothing hard-going and heavy), or a magazine where you don't have to think.

Do – ensure the bedroom is the right temperature, not too hot, and perhaps a window can be open a smidgeon to allow some fresh air in.

Do – keep the lighting low, and any natural light that might sneak in through windows minimised by blinds or curtains.

Don'ts

Don't – use your phone or tablet just before you go to bed. The light of the device will stimulate your brain to 'awake' mode, so be sure to come off any technology a good hour before sleep time to give your mind a chance to unwind.

Don't – take your phone to bed. It can be so tempting to have it near us to keep checking, use as an alarm clock, etc., but this will only cause us to be aware that it's there and can hinder our relaxation and sleep. Either turn it on to 'airplane' mode where all data will cease to ping up relentlessly, or even better, put your phone in another room where you can't see or hear it. If you *need* to be contactable during sleep hours, let whoever needs to know that you will be on a landline only and that ideally you won't be on your phone until the morning.

Don't – use your bedroom as anything other than a place to sleep. Avoid the temptation of using your bed as a sofa to watch TV, dinner table to eat dinner, etc. Keep your bedroom as a cosy sanctuary for sleep-time only, so your brain can distinguish the difference.

Don't – keep any of those worries and anxiety-inducing niggles in. Keep a pad and pen nearby your bed so you can have a good 'brain dump' before you're ready to turn in. Having things on our mind won't help our good Slow Wave sleep to do its thing effectively, so write down anything that's bothering you or needs to be done and you can pick it up again tomorrow.

ELECTRONIC FREE ZONE

Dr Reetta says...

Insomnia

I admire Anna for her honesty and how she found the courage to ask for help. How frightened and exhausted she must have been at the time, especially now that we have learnt about her insomnia. Making that first step of admitting to someone that you need help can be a tough one. Especially if you are used to 'just getting on with it' or you are someone with high expectations for yourself. Anna reached out to her mum, after a very scary sounding panic attack. Do you have people who you can turn to for support?

On the other hand, you may find yourself in a situation where someone close to you wants to talk to you about their mental health. My advice is to stay calm, don't judge, listen (and don't worry about long silences), and ask open-ended questions. You don't have to have any answers (you can find out together about any 'action points' once you have had the conversation), just being there is important.

Sometimes it's not just the lack of sleep that adds to people's anxiety levels, but it's that they *think* they haven't had enough sleep. Worrying about sleep can make it worse. Once you have established a good evening routine and attended to any physical/practical problems that might interfere with sleep (is your bed comfortable enough? Have you cut out caffeine in the evenings? Is there anything that your partner can do about their snoring?), it's time to address your thoughts and worries.

Top tips for good sleep

Top tip 1
Un-learn the habit of thinking about problems in bed. It is common for people to worry in bed, but it is not the time to do that! Make sure your bed is a place for sleep and calm only.

Top tip 2
Learn to relax in bed. Create a haven, a cosy space which will induce positive feelings, and practise the full-body relaxation techniques that Anna discusses in this chapter and in Chapter 7.

▶

Anna's activity alerts cover various ways of achieving a relaxed state when in bed. One of my favourites, that I often discuss with my clients, is relaxation through exploring your senses (Anna's 'Play it out in your head in bed' activity). When you are attending to your sleep environment by taking sensory information in through your senses, this allows you to focus on the moment rather than have your mind race through worries.

Top tip 3
Write down your thoughts and worries before you try to go to sleep, as well as any action points – once they are all on paper, you don't need to worry about forgetting them and you will be able to attend to them later.

Finally, occasionally suffering from poor sleep should not be a cause for major concern, and this is to be expected at times (e.g. before an exam, job interview). The good news is that occasional bad nights aren't thought to negatively affect performance.

5

LOW MOOD, DEPRESSION AND PTSD – THE '*LEAVE ME ALONE*' FEELING

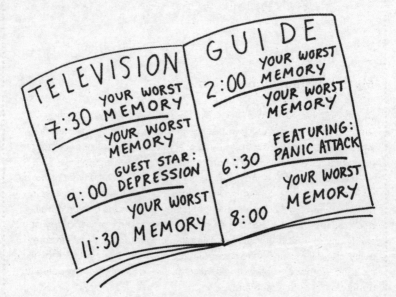

Anna's Quick Fix SOS

EASE OFF YOURSELF When we're feeling down, or generally under-par, we can be particularly hard on ourselves, when actually we should be doing the opposite. Your feelings are important and valid, so ease off being hard on yourself, and allow yourself to be kind to your needs.

DON'T ISOLATE YOURSELF It can feel so much easier to go into hibernation and cut ourselves off from others when we're feeling unable to cope. Notice if this is something that resonates with you, and in order to get support (even without actually asking for it) have a think about who you feel comfortable around, and places where you feel at ease, just so you're not alone.

EXPRESS YOURSELF Talking when we're feeling down can perhaps be the hardest things to muster up the energy to do, but it's a great way to get any pent-up emotions and thoughts out of your head. Talk to a trusted friend or write down how you're feeling as a letter to yourself perhaps ... however you do it, just get the feelings OUT.

Myth busting: 'depression'

Depression. Horrible word isn't it. The 'Great Depression', a weather 'depression' ... no matter in what sentence or circumstance it's used, the word 'depression' just seems to have overwhelming negative connotations. It's strange how a single word can conjure up such feeling isn't it?

So many people bandy around the word too, how many times have you heard someone dramatically declare, hand to forehead damsel in distress-style, 'I'm so depressed', when they've perhaps broken a nail, been dumped, or the dreaded hormones have taken over for a day or so? Many of us can be guilty of using the terminology in vain, I'm sure I'm guilty of it still at times, yet I'm certain nobody means any offence by it, it's just a word we've all become very used to, without perhaps actually appreciating its true meaning.

So, what does being 'depressed' *really* mean and feel like, and why do some of us experience it in life? Similarly to anxiety, depression currently affects 1 in 5 people in the UK. Wow, that is an extraordinary statistic isn't it? When you consider the national population is made up of nearly 65 million people, that means a staggering 13 million are allegedly suffering from depression.

There are many reasons why a person might be feeling depressed, and there are indeed many different levels. From low mood to clinical depression to bipolar disorder, just as anxiety carries many different levels of severity, the same can be said for depression, and there's a whole host of labels out there which can (wrongly) carry so much stigma (and that's a whole new can of worms).

I often have clients come to me saying they are depressed, and they may well be, however, having enquired whether this is a medical diagnosis or they've just done a quick Google search, I more often than not discover that it's an unclear self-diagnosis based on what they 'think' depression is.

It can therefore be a good idea to do a further 'self-audit' to see how you feel about a range of situations in your life to help you and your GP ascertain whether you are indeed showing signs of depression, or you're perhaps experiencing a period of low mood, stress and anxiety instead – which is also a 'thing' and can feel rubbish, it can just be more helpful to identify sooner rather than later in order to do something about it asap, without perhaps going down the often more hard core medication routes that established depression can involve.

I'm a huge believer in early intervention, and I've seen first hand the benefits that being self-aware and picking up on our mental and physical cues can give. I wish, that all those years ago, I had been more 'in tune' with myself to recognise, and do something about, the warning signs that were so clearly going off in me, so that I didn't allow the initial niggle to turn into the huge juggernaut that it did some several months later.

Causes of depression

There are no hard and fast rules when it comes to anything mental health-related I've found, particularly when it comes to low mood and depression. There isn't a 'type', depression – much as anxiety and mental health in general – doesn't discriminate, and can affect anyone at any time. Children, teens, adults, the elderly, no one is more prone to feeling it than anyone else, and it's important not to put pressure on oneself if they are feeling any low feelings, as this can only serve to make you feel worse.

I know that when I was in the grip of my anxiety and depression symptoms, I felt that I didn't 'deserve' to feel as I did, as I had nothing to be depressed about. This only made me feel worse, more pressured and even lower. I fully accept now that I was as entitled as the next man or woman to experience what I was feeling, without any guilt, shame or justification attached. I may not have (thankfully) endured years of a trauma or significant event, which some might quite rightly attribute as a 'tick box' for feeling depressed, but I had my own experiences and feelings that were just as valid as anyone else's.

I find so many people struggle to accept *why* they feel as they do. I get it, I was one of them, the fact is though that none of us choose to feel depressed, no one in their right mind would ever self-inflict such a condition, however, sometimes events can take place in life, or feelings can fester, which can end up with low mood and depressive thoughts.

There are many perhaps obvious and justified reasons why someone might experience depression at some stage in their life, and some less so obvious, and these can include:

- Life events – such as school/education issues, a traumatic event such as being mentally or physically abused or assaulted, or a work situation such as being sacked or bullied.
- Loss or bereavement – such as losing a loved one, a beloved family pet, a parent leaving/divorce, a relationship breaking down, or a major life change such as moving house, children leaving the family home, etc.
- Anger – this can be when your emotions in response to a particularly upsetting event or situation have become 'buried' internally, and the unresolved angry feelings are expressed as depression.
- Childhood experiences – such as neglect, parent issues, divorced parents, a traumatic experience, or sexual, emotional and physical abuse.

- Physical conditions – these can include conditions that affect the brain and nervous system, learning and physical disabilities, hormonal problems, sleep and poor diet.
- Medication side-effects – sometimes the after effects of an operation or certain medications can cause depressive side-effects.
- Booze and drugs – they may make you feel good momentarily, but recreational drugs and alcohol can make you feel ten times worse in the long run.
- Genes – depressive disorders can run in families, both being passed down through genetics and learned behaviour.

So you see, these are just some of the causes of depression, and there are no doubt loads more that exist which we're not even aware of yet, you may even be able to add your own. You might not even have a clue why you might be feeling low initially, and that is equally ok, just accept that that's how you feel for now, and if you feel you want to and can explore it further, that can be a great help in tackling it.

First up, let's get some self-awareness going. You can do the exercise on page 84 any time, I find it's a really good way to keep in check of yourself and can be really helpful in measuring your mood.

What depression ISN'T and how it 'feels'

As well as identifying what depression and low mood is, it's also important to note what low mood or depression *isn't*.

People who are perhaps not suffering with any of these troublesome feelings can tend to be unsure about how to understand what someone might be going through and feeling, and I find that many family members and friends can seriously misunderstand what depression is, and crucially, isn't. Based on feedback from my own research and general opinions I pick up on, I think it's important to share the common misconceptions of depression in order to help educate others, which in turn should only serve as helpful to anyone suffering.

Feeling low in mood, or having full-blown depression doesn't mean you are suddenly cursed with a contagious disease, to be steered clear of and whispered at behind wary eyes. Or that you're suddenly going to boil a pet bunny or burn down the family home! People who are feeling depressed don't need to feel any more exposed or isolated than they already do, or treated as a freak, so crossing over the road or not inviting them to a social event will only serve to perpetuate the crappy feelings of loneliness and despair.

Depression sufferers are not deliberately 'attention seeking'. I find it so unkind and disrespectful when I hear people remark that 'so-n-so' is only fishing for attention by being 'miserable'. When you're in the pits of feeling down, you physically and mentally feel done in, like you've had 10 rounds with Mike Tyson, and if you really wanted to seek attention, I bet you could think of a million other, more fun ways of doing so.

Sometimes, due to the overwhelming feelings of dread, tiredness and lack of energy, it really can feel impossible to do anything other than cope with the daily feelings that are quite frankly exhausting to deal with alone. It can take a load of effort just to live with depression. Sometimes due to these often debilitating feelings, you might find plans need to be cancelled at the last minute, or you're unable to make work one day, this doesn't mean that that person is unreliable or a liability, or being rude or a bad uncaring friend, it means they just can't do it in that moment – and believe me, they will feel all the more guilty and depressed for having to do so (when they really should be made to feel it's ok).

Depression can seem inconsistent in that some days are better than others. In fact, some days can be really good, sometimes fooling others that you're 'ok' now, only then to be followed with an 'in bed' day feeling low. Feeling depressed isn't just feeling 'a little bit sad', and something that someone can 'pull themselves together' over, or powered through. If only it were that simple. I totally get that it can be confusing trying to deal with someone who has depression, and the fact that we can't 'see' the problem I think makes it all the more frustrating – we all seem to feel more comfortable if we can identify an issue by sight or logic, thus giving us a foundation to work with – yet when it's something mental health-related, it isn't quite as obvious or easy unfortunately, and this is where we need to be more flexible with our empathy and understanding.

Activity alert

How am I now?

With the following scale, rate yourself between 1 and 10, where you feel you 'fit'. Do this each day or once a week (depending on how you're feeling – daily if you're feeling rubbish, weekly if you're just 'checking in') and use the findings to notice improvements, and/or when you need to make changes and/or get further help. This can be helpful to share with a friend, health worker or GP to help get you any relevant support.

1 feeling good, peaceful and content
2 overall feeling good, nothing niggling but if really tried, could maybe dig something up
3 a little bit down, nothing major but if I really think about it, there's something bothering me
4 mildly upset, worried, bothered to the point it's noticeable to you
5 fairly upset, to the point it's hard to ignore negative or unpleasant thoughts
6 not feeling great, feeling like something needs to be done to help you
7 feeling quite bad, am functioning but increasingly difficult to do so
8 feel terrible, no energy, can't be bothered to talk to anyone, want to be alone
9 feeling desperate, unable to cope, unsure which way to turn or what to do
10 help! Crisis point, don't know what to do, need help and support urgently

There is no hard and fast rule, cure, or quick fix for depression. Everyone is unique and different and should be treated as such with respect, yet there is a lot that can be done to help the symptoms and feelings, and in general it seems to be something that requires flexible handling and understanding. Some people have depression for years, others have a quick and happy recovery – the key is not to judge or measure anyone by anybody else.

Getting the lowdown on Post Traumatic Stress Disorder (PTSD)

Wowzers, now there's a hefty label. We can pretty much work out what Post Traumatic Stress Disorder (PTSD) is by what it says on the tin – a stressful traumatic incident which is still being 'experienced' after the event.

You might have heard this term used with regards to war veterans who have returned from conflict or war zones, having perhaps witnessed or been involved in horrific, emotionally disturbing scenes, which they haven't managed to process internally properly, and are instead left experiencing them physically, mentally and emotionally some time after the event, with the traumatic memory replaying in their mind again and again.

Shock can be a cause of this as our mind and body is brilliantly designed to stop us absorbing the full impact of traumatic event/s in the first instance they happen as we're too busy dealing with them in the here and now, however, when the danger or experience has passed, and we are in a non-threatening situation some time after, the smallest of triggers or memories can be set off like an alarm as stress hormones surge, and a part of our brain (it's called the 'amygdala' if you're interested) sends a signal to rest of our body to falsely suggest that we are still in danger – it's kind of like a panic button, or one of those essential but nuisance smoke alarms that go off at the merest whiff of burning toast.

PTSD may be diagnosed if someone has been experiencing continual fear and distress for some time after an incident, and often certain things, experiences and memories can trigger these intense feelings of terror. Smells, sounds and even completely unrelated feelings can spring up a traumatic memory, transporting the poor sufferer straight back into the event again, reliving the fear and feelings.

Often, a person will process a stressful or upsetting event in time, allowing the brain to go through the check list of emotions, rationalising any unhelpful fear and unresolved feelings, and thus leaving the memory in the past where it will stay, fully resolved and at peace with.

Sometimes this can take longer than others, but essentially working through it and processing the event can hopefully leave the sufferer in a neutral, resolved state. This is where talking can be essential.

My darling late Grandfather fought in the Second World War as a Tank Commander on the battlefields. He was so close to being killed one day by a German sniper, who missed his head with a bullet by a millimetre, that for a year after returning from the war, my Nanny said he still replayed and was 'locked in' to the memory.

Five years of living away from home, witnessing inexplicable things, with no female company around, changed him as a man for years after he returned home from the front line – something she said took years to fully process and work through to 'normality' again. Fortunately he went on to have a rich, happy and fulfilling life, but there are many who are unable to process and get rid of traumatic memories, and thus can leave people struggling with their inner self and unable to cope with everyday life – which is where PTSD, anxiety and depression are very closely linked. The high state of arousal doesn't go away as easily as it should: it's like leaving the kitchen tap on full with a broken stopcock.

Who does PTSD affect?

PTSD can also apply to situations and events that perhaps on paper aren't quite so traumatic to Joe Public, but to the person experiencing it, can be truly terrifying and gut wrenchingly traumatic.

Sufferers of PTSD can sometimes experience the condition as a result of many scenarios which are personal to them, and should never be questioned, and always respected. These can include undergoing medical procedures, witnessing an accident or death, being involved in a car accident, experiencing a difficult birth or labour, being attacked, there are many, many more reasons, but the main thread is that each incident and trigger is unique to each individual and should be treated as such.

I had a client who, while merrily driving to work one day, feeling fit as a fiddle, suddenly felt a sharp pain in her chest which then spread rapidly to her lungs, causing her breathing to fail almost instantly. She managed to pull over safely and dial the emergency services, who came within ten minutes, but during those achingly terrifying minutes waiting for help, alone, not only was she in excruciating pain, she also felt she was going to die. The paramedics arrived to find her in a petrified anxious state, and quickly assessing the situation, intervened with a particularly terrifying procedure of re-inflating the diagnosed collapsed lung. If you've ever seen *Pulp Fiction* and the scene where Uma Thurman's character 'Mia' has an adrenalin shot in the heart ... well, the ways and means of inflating my client's collapsed lung was very similar in method and brute force! Ouch!

Fortunately the medical side of this random and rogue situation was quickly stabilised, treated and signed off by the doctors, happy that this shouldn't happen again. *Un*fortunately, the emotional side-effects of the event were so traumatic that they were relived physically and mentally again and again for years afterwards by way of panic attacks, and a fear of leaving home in case it happened again.

My client went from being a vibrant happy young woman, with her whole life ahead of her, to a virtual recluse terrified of going too far from home for fear of being unsafe and the event happening again. It didn't matter that the doctors had said it was a near enough impossibility for a recurring episode to happen, the psychological damage had been done, and the levels of stress and trauma were so high and unresolved that anything which involved going in the car would spark the same feelings of panic and terror that occurred on that fateful day.

Fortunately, over time, and some brilliant intervention work from various sources, my client managed to process and understand the event, make peace with the trauma, and build new behaviours where the levels of stress and anxiety were reset to a normal setting.

If there is something, perhaps a memory or past event, that niggles or worries you to the point it stops you doing certain things, have a try with this next activity.

▶

Activity alert

Facing the fear

At all times during this activity I want you to make you stay in a 'disassociated' position – this means you are regarding the scene or situation from a distanced perspective of yourself. Imagine you're watching from afar. The aim of this is to keep any negative upsetting emotions at a comfortable distance so you can regard them calmly.

Have a think about what the situation or event was that caused these feelings of unease. From a disassociated position take yourself back in your mind to that moment, that memory, and just allow it to 'play', like a movie. You might like to close your eyes for this. ◯ It's important not to go straight back into the heart of the event, this is why we stay at a distance, I just want you to notice and feel the emotions and feelings slightly, not fully. Check that you're ok and comfortable with what you're remembering so far ◯ Take yourself to the very beginning of this memory and remember the first time you experienced the unresourceful reaction. Then I want you to take yourself back just a little bit further, to the moment just before this happened, when you were feeling calm and relaxed. Really enjoy creating and remembering this part of just before. ◯ Now, I want you have a think about how you'd like to feel *after* this memory is played again. Enjoy being really creative with this, utilising your fabulous skills of conjuring up sounds, pictures and feelings. ◯ OK, now for the really creative bit. I want you to imagine you're in your sitting room watching the TV. On the TV is a home video of your specific 'memory', on pause at the point just before, where you're feeling calm and relaxed. ◯ In your 'mind's eye', get up (taking the remote control) and walk outside the room, and close the door imagining there is a window in the door so you can look in still. Now, you should be standing just outside the sitting room, looking through the window in the door into the room where you can clearly see the TV on pause ready to go. ◯ Now, press 'play' on the remote and allow your memory to play out, from the moment just before the event, right through to the end. As the video is playing, notice that the sound quality and picture is not great, in fact it's terrible ... crackly, inaudible, fuzzy ... like there's a storm outside and there's interference. As it gets worse, notice how the image is getting smaller, duller, the sounds fading.

▶

Remember you are watching this from outside the room, looking in. ○ As you reach the end of the video, which is now fuzzy and quiet, I want you to press 'rewind' on the remote control and whizz the home video all the way back through to the beginning, right to point just before the memory started again, where you were feeling calm and relaxed. Enjoy that feeling, make it as good as it can be, colourful, feeling fabulous, and take a nice deep breath. ○ From that disassociated position behind the door, repeat, 5 times, the process of playing through the home video, with the picture and sound all mushy and distorted, and then quickly rewind to the very beginning, making each time you get to the start more and more alluring and wonderful. ○ Once you've given that a good go, and each time should come easier and easier, notice how you feel, embracing the strong empowered feelings of just before. Lock them in and ask yourself how you're feeling about that memory/ event now? ○ Keep practising this as and when you need to and each time congratulating yourself on being in control of your memories and emotions. The brain is most obedient and does as we tell and show it, the more we experience the good 'before' feelings, and rubbish the unresourceful memory to the point of it being unrecognisable, the better we can feel in general about anything that causes us upset.

My story

I was never actually diagnosed with full-blown PTSD, but I certainly felt the effects of the trauma and 'cycle of fear' from experiencing my first panic attack. Certain times of the day, particularly night time, would spark feelings of dread, panic and terror, and little things such as the smell of certain aftershaves (my ex's scent) would set off the 'panic alarm' in my brain as I unconsciously recalled the isolated incident of having my first major panic attack. So, there were definitely symptoms of trauma from a significant situation affecting me way after the event.

A combination of permanently high levels of stress for far too long a time, which comprised of a mixture of low mood, mild depression, anxiety and trauma, all went hand in hand with my condition and how I presented my anxiety disorder. When I break it all down, I can really see how and why I felt the way I did. At the time I felt like a freak, a total weirdo and lost cause ... now I feel, blimey ... no wonder I couldn't cope with all that going on!

There are still times, even now, if I'm particularly tired or when I'm staying away from home alone where I feel the old familiar feelings creep back in. I believe this stems from that original panic attack and trauma when I felt very isolated, alone and exhausted. Habits can be hard to break, but I am living proof that a good dose of understanding and working to change, can make all the difference to overcoming life's challenges.

And finally

There might be times when you just really can't be bothered. Days when the mood is just stuck in a rut, the black hole, and that's ok. Sometimes taking all pressure to be Mr or Miss Perky away can be hugely beneficial. Allowing yourself to have an off day is perfectly fine, just be aware of how you're feeling and keep checking in on yourself. Any longer than a few days, and/or if you're starting to feel worse, don't suffer alone, do think about seeing your GP for help, exploring one of the many specialised agencies and charities such as Mind and The Samaritans, and talking to someone you trust to offload and share how you're feeling.

Activity alert

Challenge it, change it

Car manufacturer, Henry Ford, once said, 'whether you think you can or think you can't, you're right' – I think this is such a good saying and, in my opinion, absolutely true.

There is a lot to be said for the power of the mind, and far from positive affirmations being something 'happy clappy' or sneered at by the narrow minded, there is actually a lot of scientific fact in embracing them.

Our subconscious mind is very obedient, and does not process negatives. So instead of saying, '*I don't want to feel sad today*', try saying '*I will feel happy today*'. The meaning is the same, but if you say the former sentence, all the brain picks up on are the words 'don't' and 'sad'... it cares not about the order or intention, all it hears and responds to are the words.

Challenge any negative thoughts. Find the opposite and turn any negative sentences, sayings or feelings into positive ones. So anything which starts with 'I can't' ... try and flip it to a new thought starting with 'I can'.

Turn the tide on any string of negative thoughts and/or behaviour, and nip in the bud anything repetitive which isn't serving you well, i.e., if you keep saying to yourself, '*I'll never have a relationship and no one fancies me*', then all you're doing is projecting that thought pattern out there. Remember the unconscious mind, it does as you ask, and it will happen. Try challenging such thoughts and replacing with something more uplifting, i.e. '*I deserve to find the right partner for me and it will happen when I'm ready.*'

Dr Reetta says...
Low mood, depression and PTSD

Anna writes about people's experiences of depression being unique and different. The diagnostic criteria cover so many symptoms that there may indeed be very little in common between those diagnosed with it. Because depression may not be the same for everyone, it is always essential to explore each individual's ideas of what *their* depression is. For example, there are interesting differences in how people across cultures experience depression, and it is thought that people from non-Western cultures emphasise physical symptoms (e.g. pain and fatigue) rather than psychological symptoms (e.g. feelings of guilt and thoughts about wanting to die).

What I hear in my work is that depression often creeps up on people. This often involves them stopping going out and withdrawing. When people become depressed, they first give up the 'good things' in life. What have you given up when you have felt low or depressed? I often start therapy with my clients by thinking about pleasurable or enjoyable things they can introduce into their lives, as well as how they can be kinder to themselves. Being able to reward or treat yourself is one of the key tools in improving your mental wellbeing.

Top tips for tackling low mood and depression

Top tip 1
So, have a think, what are the things that you enjoy, that help you relax or make you laugh? Think of small things, big things, things that you can buy now, things that you can save up for, things that you can say to yourself, things that you can ask others to join you with and things that you can do on your own. Perhaps over time you can learn to replace some of the critical thoughts with recognising where you have done well or at least tried hard.

▶

Top tip 2

I find it useful thinking about strategies for depression in two categories: short-term strategies to help you out of depression, and long-term strategies to reduce your chances of depression returning. Some ideas for short-term strategies are: increasing activity levels, challenging thought patterns, and considering who is around to support you. In planning how to prevent a future episode of depression, your long-term strategies, think about any improvements that are needed in the areas of diet, sleep and exercise; be kind to yourself (see earlier), and commit to building and putting effort into good relationships.

PTSD

With regard to PTSD, as Anna says, talking can be essential. In addition to 're-experiencing' the trauma, avoidance and increased arousal, people often experience a variety of feelings such as anger, confusion, guilt and shame in the months or years after a traumatic event. In working with traumatised clients, the importance of the client having someone listen to their story and believing it cannot be underestimated. Of course there are many processes and therapeutic techniques that are used to help people process their trauma, but two (or more!) people meeting together and making sense of the experiences is a very important first step.

Top tip 3

Talking with people who have gone through similar experiences is also something that many find useful. Check online if there is a support group locally for you?

If there is a traumatic experience in your past that seems to be affecting you, then have a think whether you are ready to address it. If you are, Anna's 'Facing the fear' activity alert is a good starting point. For some, who have experienced trauma, 'self-help' is all they need, but for some, professional help is required. It is very important to seek help and advice if your symptoms have been there for many months, you feel your life is not worth living, or you feel you are a risk to yourself or anyone else.

6

SELF 'HELP' MEDICATING – THE *'I CAN'T COPE'* FEELING

Anna's Quick Fix SOS

BE AWARE Turning to a substance or addictive behaviour can often become a 'go to' reaction when we're feeling the heat from anxiety or depression to mask the overwhelming feelings. Notice if and when you're reaching for a 'coping aid' – when we're aware, it's harder to hide.

SEEK SUPPORT AND TELL SOMEONE Many people feel embarrassed or ashamed if they are using alternative methods of coping which aren't perhaps socially accepted, or even legal, in society. Be brave, you aren't to blame and deserve love and support, seek someone you trust to confide in and help break the destructive behaviour.

BE KIND TO YOURSELF Try not to judge yourself or speak badly to yourself about what's happening. If you are self-medicating it's usually because you need and want a rest and escape from the awful feelings. It's not your fault, and the more you feel shame or negative feelings about yourself, the harder it can become. You most probably didn't ask for this, so be kind to you.

What, when, why?

For me, self-medicating conjures up a rather dark and depressing scene, like that iconic image from the 90s movie *Trainspotting* where Ewan McGregor does all he can to get his 'fix', following his agitation and need to do whatever he has to do to 'get it', to the visible release and relief as his actions have their desired effect. His substance of choice was heroin, pretty hardcore stuff, and one could argue, was he self-medicating an underlying feeling of lacking to cope, or just satisfying his drug addiction? Well, it could be seen as exactly the same thing, and when it comes to anxiety and depressive disorders, self-medicating can be a 'go to' cure in desperation at not being able to handle scary and overwhelming feelings.

Of course *Trainspotting* is only a film, but self-medicating with a substance or behaviour, is very real indeed.

What?

So, what does 'self-medicating' actually mean? Who does it? How and when? Well, the answer is, anyone can reach a point when they think the only option for them, at that time, is to numb the feelings or situation they're feeling. Ways of doing this include reaching for an alcoholic drink, drugs (prescriptive and illegal), or partaking in an addictive behaviour such as over/under eating, gambling or sexual behaviour, for example.

Now, to be clear, I'm not suggesting for one moment that *all* people suffering with alcohol dependencies, or whatever their 'go to' crutch, have an underlying anxiety disorder, but what I *am* saying is that a lot of people unwittingly hide what is perhaps an undiagnosed mental health issue with a 'cover up comfort blanket' of self-medicating. It's often a gradual process, something which perhaps starts small or infrequent, and then spirals out of control so the original issue is perhaps sidelined, and becomes a whole new, bigger one, in the form of a potential or actual addiction.

In this chapter, for ease of context, I'll be mainly shedding some light on self-medicating through alcohol and recreational drugs, and certain behaviours such as sexual habits and gambling. I'll be going into more detail on the use of prescription medication in Chapter 7, exercise and eating issues in Chapter 8, and self-harm in Chapter 9, which can all come under the self-medicating umbrella.

When?

Many people cope just fine with day-to-day stresses and the often challenging events that make up our lives. We've all been there at the end of a particularly irksome day (I know I have) where we come home and all we want to do is grab the nearest bottle of plonk and pour a vast glass to gulp gratefully, the stresses and strains of the day slightly ebbing away as the 'medicinal' effects of the booze take hold. Let's be honest, there really is nothing better than a 'drink drink' after a long day at the grindstone.

However, if this seemingly innocent and widely accepted, even celebrated, habit turns into more of a 'need', and then 'I really need', and then 'I can't cope without', it becomes a problem.

It's one thing having a glass of your favourite tipple once in a while, particularly if we crave some instant gratification from the calming, numbing effects, after all a 'snifter' or 'stiff drink' has been used and widely accepted for years as a way of dealing with shock, stress or nerves (however unhelpfully), but it's when that occasional, every now and then drink, starts to become a tad more frequent, habitual, and tellingly when the habit starts to control and choose you, as opposed to the other way round anymore – that's a cause for concern.

You don't have to drink or use all day from the moment you wake to be considered an 'addict', in fact often people will justify their actions by using this excuse at first by saying *'I can't have a dependency because I don't need it all the time'*, however, if the self-medicating gets to a stage where it's happening to a point where you can't stop it by choice, it's become an issue that shouldn't be ignored.

The 'solution' to your stress and anxiety can slip into dependency, and before you know it the dependency has turned into addiction, with a whole new series of problems – probably more troubling than the reason for the drink in the first place, i.e. anxiety, stress, gets buried as a secondary issue, as the addiction takes over as the presenting dominant problem. Once a using pattern begins, often innocently enough, it can tend to have a life of its own and a pathway of self-destruct can often follow.

Why?

So, why does it happen? Why do some of us turn to self-medicating and others don't? The answer to that unfortunately isn't clear-cut, there is no 'type' of person, much as the way mental health doesn't discriminate, the same can be said for those who find themselves on the slippery slope to self-medicating.

Those stressful days I was talking about, well if they start to become more and more built up with no opportunity to release the pressures and strains in a healthy way, i.e. communicating, time out, then the feelings are going to build up like a pressure cooker. Anxiety might present itself physically by way of panic attacks, low mood, social anxiety, feeling worried permanently, or the mind might start to feel 'full' and race full of worries and exhausting thoughts, so what might we decide to do? Aha ... reach for a calming drink, drug or behaviour, to help the intensity go away.

You may have experienced a particularly upsetting or traumatic event and the memory keeps replaying in your mind – the desire for a quick fix release from the feelings is welcomed. Perhaps you're feeling isolated and unable to communicate effectively with someone to offload your day-to-day thoughts and feelings – the appeal of something to numb the feelings and boost confidence, mood or self-esteem can be ever more appealing.

I totally get all this, I was partial to the odd glass of wine of an evening during my initial pre-diagnosed anxiety disorder (thankfully it didn't get out of hand), but it's important to remember that the effects of your medication of choice are only temporary, and are almost certain to create even more problems down the line.

Prevention and early intervention to avoid going down this route is key.

Who can it happen to?

I felt it was really important to include this chapter in my book as it's an area of mental health that often gets brushed under the carpet, misunderstood, and in my experience, both professionally and personally, can be a massive part of dealing with anxiety.

I've met a lot of people who've felt ashamed, embarrassed and desperate as a result of turning to self-medicating to help cope with an underlying anxiety issue. What starts out as an innocent drink, smoking some weed or using pornographic websites or gambling, for example, as a way to relax and mask the overwhelming feelings of anxiety or low mood, can over time bleed into a need, and then a dependency.

Drowning our sorrows, or burying our stress by necking a bottle or two of liquor, or getting a 'fix', can initially hit the spot, it can feel good and ease off the severity of the anxiety 'claw' as it papers over the cracks, but as we all know from those nights when we've perhaps over indulged and had one too many, the next day, or even several days after, we can feel totally rubbish and melancholy. What started out as a brilliant night, full of confidence flinging yourself around a dance floor, downing shot after shot of some unnaturally neon liquid, buoyed up by the booze or drugs, can very quickly hours later feel like a huge vat of bricks has been poured right over your head, rendering you horizontal and feeling as rough as a badger's butt.

There's a reason for that, not only the bad quality of sleep we will undoubtedly have had from being under the influence (we may pass out but it's never a 'quality' sleep), but also, alcohol and drugs have depressive side-effects and can be totally counterproductive if you've been using them to feel better in the first place – you've heard the saying, *what goes up must come down*', and that is never truer than when the effects of substances wear off, the term of experiencing a 'come down' is extremely accurate.

Now, if you've been using that substance of choice to mask any inner feelings of anxiety, stress or low mood, once the initial 'high' has worn off, you'll more often than not end up feeling worse, with the original feeling back with a vengeance and causing you more grief than before due to the exhaustion, and withdrawal kicking in. To be frank, at this point you're in a right pickle and this is where the alarm bells should be ringing off the hook.

So, what might you do? Well, there are a couple of paths ... you might realise how terrible you feel and that you never want to feel like this again, so you're not going to do 'that' again and explore other, more healthy, helpful ways to tackle any underlying issues. Or, you might decide that you feel so horrific and anxious/depressed/stressed that you need some respite asap, and so you reach for that double-edged sword once again, the one thing that put you in this predicament in the first ▶

Activity alert

Pattern detective diary

In this exercise the key is to be really honest with yourself – if you find you're not, that can be telling in itself. We are trying to notice any negative patterns emerging and giving yourself a great opportunity to get a grip on what's going on day to day, week to week, in order to help break any concerning, impulsive and compulsive behaviour.

Find something to write your findings in – either a piece of paper, a diary, a chalkboard, post it notes by the bed, smartphone, etc. ⊙ Jot down Monday to Sunday on your chosen material, and leave enough room to write any details by each entry. ⊙ Make a deal with yourself that you're going to chart your mood, behaviour and habits for the next 7 days. Be really honest with yourself and remind yourself why you're doing this, and what it will give you. ⊙ Each day, as you go about your business, write down as you go, or at the end of the day as a whole; your activities, your mood, how you're feeling, what you're eating and drinking, and, if it applies, taking. ⊙ Notice what you're doing, and crucially, when. Is there a certain time of the day you feel a particular way? Reach for a certain 'crutch' to help you through? Do something habitual? ⊙ Be honest and clear with yourself, and write it all down. The impact of seeing something written down can be hugely helpful when we want to change and/or take notice. It can be the kick in the right direction we sometimes need. ⊙ Continue noting down your behaviours, feelings, etc. for the whole week, then after the 7 days are up, take a moment to have a good look back over the week that has been, reading and noting all you have written. Notice if any patterns are emerging i.e. your behaviour, mood, feelings, or times when you can't cope and need help from a substance or certain behaviour. ⊙ If you feel brave enough, and you should because you are being brilliantly honest and open with yourself, have a think about sharing your findings with a trusted friend, or if you feel there is a much more pressing issue that's emerged, your GP for further support. ⊙ Sometimes, just by taking responsibility for ourselves, taking that control back and doing something about any worrying behaviour, can be a huge help in nipping anything unhelpful in the bud, before it gets out of hand.

WOW things are really difficult and awful

AND I don't want to deal with any of this AT ALL

I know!

let's watch tv and ignore EVERYTHING

place, but gave you that temporary release, and wait for the effects to kick in.

Of course, you're an intelligent human being, and you know that the right course of action is the first one, but it's not always as simple as that, particularly if you're in the grips of anxiety. Unfortunately if you're not sure where or who to go to, how to get help, or indeed that there IS help out there, you might opt for the latter, and there a whole new catalogue of problems can unfold.

It can be the hardest thing in the world to gain some clarity at times like this, and to make the 'right' choices. If only it were that easy. It's rarely easy, let's be clear about that, but you do have the inner strength and self-control to be able to make the decisions you need to – after all, there's only one person in charge of you and your future … you.

If you're feeling in this quandary and not sure which way to turn, have a go at the next exercise to help bring some well-formed decisions into play and to gain some clarity and balance.

Lifting the lid on the taboo

The connection between mental health and self-medicating is something which isn't spoken about nearly enough for my liking. There is such a taboo surrounding it, a hidden shame or dirty little secret, when really anyone felt compelled to have to administer their own kind of unregulated 'self-help' should be given nothing but support and sympathy.

Of course, in many situations it can be hard to see the wood from the trees, as the root cause of such behaviour, or 'coping mechanism', can go undetected by those nearest and dearest, and instead, the 'perpetrator' is seen as being a handful, destructive and 'with issues'. There is much evidence, sadly, that suggests for every one person locked in a bitter cycle of self-medicating, there are several loved ones, often family members, on the sidelines also suffering.

Living with, being married to, or knowing someone who is seeking help through unhelpful means, can be utterly devastating for all involved. Often the illness, for at this point the self-medicating is an illness in itself, is disguised or masked. The addiction can morph into strange behaviour such as fabricating the truth, mood changes such as being on edge and irritable, a lack of social skills (withdrawn, no eye contact), or indeed an overuse of them (lairy and aggressive), and the person's physical appearance may also change, perhaps puffy, unkempt and poor personal hygiene, rapid weight loss, red face, sunken eyes … all are clues that perhaps all is not well.

It's at this point that those surrounding, and indeed the sufferer themselves, forget who or what traits the person had in the first place, as the addictive side-effects of the self-medicating take over.

▶

Activity alert

Shoulda, woulda, coulda

Thinking clearly when we're perhaps in a bit of a pre or post self-medicating 'fog' can be tricky. Tricky, but not impossible. Read these 4 questions to yourself, and answer them as honestly and fully as you can to gain some clarity and leverage to make the 'right' choice for you. It can be hugely helpful working out what's inspiring or blocking you into making a decision – I also find it really liberating. The double negative questions ('What WOULDN'T happen if you DIDN'T do...?') are the ones you might find most challenging. This series of questions are based on an NLP technique called Cartesian questioning. The aim is to evoke different thought patterns and gain perspective from differing angles.

Using the theme around self-medicating, I want you to insert your 'thing' of choice into the question/statement to make it relevant and personal to you. You can have a play around with the focal point to change the perspective and end goal.

I've given you a hypothetical example in brackets, personal to me, to help it make sense:

○ What WOULD happen if you DID do... [insert here]?
  (e.g. What WOULD happen if I DID get help for drinking?
  'I could tackle the horrible feelings and start to feel better')

○ What WOULD happen if you DIDN'T do...[insert here]?
  (e.g. What WOULD happen if I DIDN'T get help for my drinking?
  'I would get worse, feel awful and upset everyone around me')

○ What WOULDN'T happen if I DID do...[insert here]?
  (e.g. What WOULDN'T happen if I DID get help for my drinking?
  'I wouldn't continue to feel as bad as I do now with my physical and mental health deteriorating. I wouldn't feel so alone')

▶

◯ What WOULDN'T happen if I DIDN'T do...[insert here]?
   (e.g. What WOULDN'T happen if I DIDN'T get help for my drinking?
   'I wouldn't have a chance at living a happy and fulfilled life, which
   I deserve')

The purpose of this activity is to give you a chance to explore and reflect on
the different viewpoints you've created just by asking these simple, yet
loaded, questions. Have a think about how it's made you feel and if it's
motivated you in any way to do anything different.

It's at this point that the actual 'reason' they are in this situation in the first place is perhaps forgotten ... or not even been realised, as the presenting 'behaviour' takes over opinion.

I had a wonderful client, Sarah*, who spent years self-medicating with alcohol and drugs – cheap wine and cannabis ('weed') – was her choix de jour. Five years of drinking and smoking vast quantities had left her a broken woman. It was so sad to see, and my heart went out to her. To the outside world, she had evolved into a 'waste of space', someone who lied, stole, was unreliable and unable to work, and someone who spent most of her days cooped up in her sitting room watching daytime TV as she just couldn't face anything else.

Five years previously to this, Sarah had been a successful and popular employee, she'd had a boyfriend and a loving family, a healthy social life, money, a love of fitness, and the world in front of her. It was around this time that she was involved in a car accident, which frightened and mentally traumatised her. Her physical injuries were identified and treated at the time, however, it was the ones inside, her thoughts, feelings and emotions, which were left unchallenged and treated, that were to be her downfall.

Over the next few years, the initial shock and sympathy from others gradually ebbed away to normality as the car incident became a distant memory – for everyone else, but not for Sarah. Over time, she began to be haunted and frightened by the fears of going out in a car again, and history repeating itself. She started to experience heightened anxiety, panic attacks crept in, one after another until they occurred at the mere mention of going out, and she gradually began to stay in more, her home becoming her sanctuary of safety, but also her prison.

At times she had no choice but to go out, to get food and supplies, and each time the anxiety would get so bad she would suffer silently and alone, not knowing what to do, until the day she thought a 'good stiff drink' might ease up the fear. She was right. One massive gulp from a bottle of wine she had knocking about in her kitchen instantly made the anxiety pangs lessen, she drank some more, and the fear lessened still. 'Brilliant! A solution to help me feel better', she thought. For that instant moment, it worked.

You can probably guess where this story went. Yep, it spiralled out of control. Very quickly, Sarah needed more and more booze to help her feel less anxious, and to give her the courage to function/go about daily activities, as her tolerance to her substance of choice increased. She introduced smoking weed to help take the edge off the anxiety even more, and before she knew it, the need and dependency had her in its grip. Each day she'd wake, in the midst of a post booze/drugs haze, feeling increasingly shaky, scared, panicked ... and in need of some help ... so she reached for the bottle and a joint once again.

Sarah went from being a bright healthy young lady, to an anxiety riddled addict. I can only imagine how things might have been different for her if she'd had the help she desperately needed at the time of the car accident, not five years down the line when she was sent for a severe detox in rehab in order to save her life.

Because Sarah felt unable to identify what was wrong and work through her unresolved feelings relating to the car crash (trauma), she didn't actually know who to turn to for help. Family wanted to help but without a clue as to what the underlying issue was, they were as helpless as she felt. Over the years of battling the anxiety and self-medicating, her job, friendships and family relationships suffered under the strain of coping, and her physical health took a pretty hefty nose dive to boot.

I appreciate Sarah's story might come across as rather hard hitting, and it's meant to. It's not designed to scaremonger or preach – the complete opposite in fact, as I want to REALLY demonstrate to you how a 'simple' case of untreated anxiety, which could potentially have been nipped in the bud with some talking therapy or a good pal's shoulder to cry on, way back when it first happened, can quickly take a very different path – one which serves as an often much worse additional problem. Too many people are left feeling ashamed and confused as a result of covering up an anxiety disorder with destructive behaviour, and quite frankly it isn't fair.

Finally reaching rock bottom, and you know what they say, the only way is up, following an excellent therapy programme, which dealt with the addiction and the underlying causes combined, I'm delighted to share with you that Sarah is now well, happy and back to her former best – and through choice, is teetotal. Sure, she has off days, but she knows how to handle them, and most importantly, she knows how to handle herself. She also knows how to communicate with her family and friends to let them know how she's feeling – something she wasn't quite sure of back in the car accident days.

If you or a friend or family member are concerned that you might be self-medicating, or the urge is bubbling away, this handy 'checklist' might be of use to be mindful of, and/or share with someone you love and trust who might benefit from its honesty and clarity:

7 Signs of spiralling to self-medicating to look out for

- 1 – you're feeling a bit down, under par. Every day is becoming a chore, you're not enjoying much, if anything at all, and everyday tasks and communication are starting to stress you unnecessarily. You're increasingly feeling unable to cope.
- 2 – The introduction of a few drinks, or a dabble in drugs, or a release from discovering a new behaviour, such as gambling or sex ... JUST to feel a bit better. Ooh, we discover it works. We're feeling a little better, less anxious, stressed or down.
- 3 – We fancy trying that drink/drug/behaviour again, we have evidence that tells us it helped and took the edge off the feelings. We start to rely on it as our 'go to' for help. The dependency is kicking in.
- 4 – The addiction starts to dictate our day-to-day behaviour. It becomes a part of the day. The shame or embarrassment of 'needing' this starts to get internalised and hidden from public view or opinion. The master of disguise, cover up job begins.
- 5 – The dependency is in full swing, we no longer have a clear grip on what the original problem is as we allow the addiction to do the job of numbing the feelings and taking over your mind and body, often with little care or consideration for others or indeed ourselves. We stop functioning consciously as the self-medicating does the job for us.

- 6 – The steady self-destruct is in full swing. Shame, fear, embarrassment of the self-medicating, and any consequential behaviour, is all consuming, as well as the original anxiety or depression added to the mix.
- 7 – Addiction takes over as the shame and pain needs medicating more and more to ease it. As the use increases, the anxiety, fear and pain increases, the self-honesty disappears even further away and the denial increases. The presenting behaviour is a concern for all.

Be brave, help is out there

I appreciate some of this chapter may come across a little hard hitting and heavy at times. My intention isn't to scaremonger or, heaven forbid, induce any unnecessary worry, but over the past decade of living with, exploring and dealing with people with anxiety disorders, it never fails to shock me how stigmatised those that have, through no fault of their own, found themselves at the bitter bottom of the effects of self-medicating.

I've only touched on certain coping behaviours, but as I briefly mentioned at the beginning of this chapter, there are many more that can creep under this umbrella, including self-harm (more about this in Chapter 9) and destructive behaviour such as eating disorders (see Chapter 8 for more on this), or in some cases, even inflicting abuse on another person can be loosely determined a form of 'self-medicating'.

The more we, as society, accept and help those who find themselves down this path, instead of judging and throwing a withering look of disgust, the better the world would be for all – I believe that anyway. With 1 in 4 of us experiencing a mental health issue at some point in our life, it stands to reason that it's perhaps a much more common thing than people would like to realise. I get it, it's not the most pretty, sexy or fun thing to entertain, but it's REAL life, and the more empathy and self-help we can offer, the better chance we have to ensure suffering is kept to a minimum.

And finally, if this chapter has touched you personally, or someone you know perhaps, maybe it's resonated with how you might be feeling or what you're experiencing – fear not, you're not alone. It can feel mighty lonely and scary when we're unsure how to broach the topic of how we're feeling, but in my experience, help is out there. People aren't always mind readers so we have to be brave, give them a clue, and ask sometimes in order to get the ball rolling. Think of someone you trust to talk to, check out some of the brilliant websites such as Mind for where to get help, try your GP ... just telling someone how you're feeling can make all the difference in getting that early help, before it perhaps ends up way down at the bottom of a beer barrel.

You can do it. I believe in you.

Dr Reetta says...
Self-medicating

Self-medicating can be viewed as a 'negative stress management technique' or a 'solution' for anxiety. Whether people recognise the underlying stress or anxiety is another matter. It may bring a short-term solution, but long term it is likely to contribute to worsening of the problem, and lead to avoiding the cause of the anxiety. Many don't realise that the withdrawal symptoms (such as anxiety, insomnia, low mood) are often very similar to the symptoms that lead to people engaging in self-medicating in the first place.

If you think about an iceberg, you only see a part of it, in this case the self-medicating behaviour. It's what's underneath the sea level that most likely involves some form of anxiety. It can be hidden from everyone, including yourself. Why is it important to recognise it if it's hidden?

Top tips to tackle self-medicating

Top tip 1

Recognising and acknowledging it are the first steps to dealing with it. Anna's 'Pattern detective diary' will help you with this. You may not like the patterns you uncover, but this is the ideal starting point to starting to break your 'bad' habit, and thinking about adding some 'positive stress management techniques' to your life.

Top tip 2

What could you do instead that offers the same type of results? Could you turn your self-medicating behaviour to 'self-soothing' behaviour? It could be running, cycling, yoga, meditation, mindfulness, gardening, DIY, fishing, cooking, music, playing an instrument, art, knitting – any activity that long term could add pleasure/relaxation to your life.

Anna described her client, Sarah, whose self-medicating behaviours went on for many years before she accessed help. Timing and accessing

▶

help as early as possible is something that I often think about in my work with children and young people, especially when I successfully help them address their anxiety. Empowering a child to develop a 'toolkit' for anxiety management hopefully teaches them the idea of adapting and adding to those skills as they grow older, allowing them the lifelong skills in managing anxiety in later years – as well as teaching them that it's ok to talk about anxiety. Unfortunately, parents don't always seek help for their children's mental health problems – often due to stigma. This is a very important fact, as about half of all mental health problems, including anxiety, start in childhood. You can find more information on children and anxiety in the appendix on page 178.

7

ACHES, PAINS AND THE PHYSICAL STUFF – THE *'EVERYTHING HURTS'* FEELING

Anna's Quick Fix SOS

CONTROL YOUR BREATHING By far the most essential thing to do to relax yourself and to get the body and mind working together properly, and calmly.

DISTRACT YOURSELF Take some time out and 'get off the wheel' for a moment to focus on doing something 'else'. Exercise, a calming hobby, a completely different activity to your norm ... by physically distracting yourself and engaging in something else, can really help in calming down and reducing any physical symptoms of anxiety.

SAY 'NO' TO STRESS Sometimes easier said than done, but when we recognise that we are stressed, and that the physical symptoms of anxiety are being exacerbated as a result, we can do something about reducing any stress and therefore the physical feelings too.

Let's get 'physical'

As we know, anxiety very much comes under the umbrella of mental health, after all it's something we can experience as mentally and emotionally challenging symptoms, as has been highlighted all throughout this book, however, there is a very real physical side to anxiety too.

Many moons ago when I first started noticing my feelings of dread and anxiety, I really did feel at times that I was *physically* unwell, and that that was the actual cause of why I was feeling so internally rubbish too. In fact, the complete opposite was true, I was feeling so mentally wrung out, that my body was giving me physical clues that all was not well. And thank goodness it did!

It's a bit of a catch-22 isn't it? Are we feeling anxious *because* we're feeling physically unwell, or is the anxiety causing a physical reaction?

To be honest, both scenarios can exist, and indeed a combination of the two, and I've seen first hand the quandary people are in when they're unsure just what has exacerbated what! It's a chicken and egg conundrum.

Recognising that *something* is up, is our first warning sign and amber light that we perhaps need to sit up and take notice of ourselves – and that means both our internal and external health. I'll be shedding some more light about the fabulous ways in how we can be the best we can be physically and mentally in the next chapter, but for now, let's get to the bottom of those horrible and often debilitating physical feelings that anxiety can bring along for the ride.

The connection between physical and mental health is not made or respected nearly enough for my liking, they are intrinsically linked when it comes to anxiety symptoms. Neither one is more or less important than the other, both include extremities from the trivial to the traumatic, and it's a huge national crusade from mental health campaigners like myself to give both aspects of our health equal status, understanding and attention. As I've said in earlier chapters, with 1 in 4 of us experiencing a mental health issue at any one time, the stats and impact are surely too huge for us to think otherwise.

Unfortunately, as 'mental health' is steeped in negative stigma and draconian stereotypes of austere lunatic asylums, straight jackets, padded cells and dangerous psychopaths – we've all seen the movies – it's taken a while for common sense to catch up to remind us that it's not all like that, and for us to respect and understand *both* our physical and mental health. They make up separate parts of who we are, but they are also beautifully linked. Mental health *should* have the same stigma-free status and understanding as physical health, after all there are varying degrees of both, but unfortunately, we're still some way away from that being the norm.

To give you an idea of what I mean, and how we often place more acceptance on physical health, so many people feel more comfortable saying they've got a stomach ache and feel dizzy (the physical symptom), than the fact they're suffering from crippling unease, fear and anxiety (the mental symptom) – the feelings of anxiety are experienced *both* physically and mentally and yet we're more at ease hiding behind just the physical symptoms. Society has made us feel more accepting of a physical problem, than a mental health one, and I find that worrying and sad.

So, what can we do about it? By educating ourselves and others about how physical and mental health are actually connected, and importantly so, I believe we can, and will, go a long way to helping everyone feel more comfortable about the whole thing. We can do this!

Recognising the signs

Each year hundreds, thousands of people rush to hospital in agony and fear thinking they're having a heart attack. I hear it so often. Their chest is tight, they're in pain, can't breathe, and of course for some unlucky souls they are of course having a cardiac arrest of sorts, however, for a vast majority of people what they are in fact having is a panic or anxiety attack. No less scary I hasten to add, but fortunately far less life threatening – in fact, as we know, a panic attack alone cannot kill you.

So it just goes to show how *physical* experiencing a form of anxiety can be. It's a powerful, visceral reaction. There are many other physical ways we can experience anxiety, and these can include:

- shoulder pain
- stomach ulcers
- headaches
- migraines
- achy limbs
- throat issues including swallowing (dysphagia) and lump sensations (globus)
- pins and needles
- dizziness
- tummy aches
- gut and bowel issues such as Irritable Bowel Syndrome (IBS)
- general aches and pains, sometimes isolated to an area.

There are several things we can do about this. Firstly, it's vitally important you visit your GP or medical professional to share what you might be experiencing, just for peace of mind and to rule out anything which might

my mind
feels like
a mess

and my
body feels
like a mess too

another
winning
combination!

benefit from further investigation. Internet diagnosis is never recommended as a way of deciphering what might be wrong, there are so many conflicting suggestions and unhelpful incorrect scaremongering that it's best to steer well clear, particularly for those prone to anxiety ... not a good mix ... so always make sure you nobble your doctor instead for a proper examination and medical opinion before you even *think* about reaching for an internet search engine.

We can also use relaxation and breathing skills to reduce the physical feelings we might be experiencing. Often the physical symptoms of anxiety can be so intense, which is exactly what is happening ... we are tensing up our bodies. Think of it as a coiled-up spring, it has been wound and wound up such that it's so taut there is no 'give'. Tension has a direct connection to experiencing certain feelings of physical discomfort. How many of us have needed the loo, and I mean *really* needed the loo, with excruciating tummy gripes and all, in times of feeling stressed or tense? And how often do people get 'tension' headaches and a stiff neck, back and shoulders from feeling anxious and stressed? Personally I've ticked every box over the years.

I'll take you through one of my favourite relaxation exercises in a moment, which should help 'turn down' the severity of physical anxiety, but first I wanted to flag other ways in which some people deal with the physical symptoms of anxiety, and when we need to be really careful and clued up about not taking things too far.

Popping a pill for pain

In the previous chapter, I've talked about self-medicating, particularly with alcohol, illegal drugs and certain behaviours, and when we need to be aware of taking (literally) a destructive and unhelpful path to coping with anxiety.

Physical pain and discomfort is often coupled with 'taking something' to deal with the pain. In many cases that is of course a sensible course of action. After all, if we've got a headache it's fairly standard practice to reach for an Ibuprofen or paracetamol, or if we've had an operation, for example, or are experiencing a more severe pain or illness, something stronger from the doctor such as Tramadol or OxyContin can be prescribed.

However, there are times when the automatic reach for a pill is in fact just masking the underlying cause of the pain, perhaps emotionally as well as physically, perhaps there is even no pain present at all, we just like the numbing, relaxing or euphoric effects the pills induce, and we can fall blindly into a dangerous self-medicating pattern of behaviour.

Painkiller abuse and addiction is a 'thing', and is increasingly becoming a huge concern due to the ease of obtaining medication. The fact it is legal makes it more 'acceptable' and disguisable, under the pretence that you need it just for pain relief. You only have to check the media to read stories of celebrities who have gravely come unstuck as a result of taking a concoction of strong prescribed, and over-the-counter medications, which are highly addictive. Often taking something which has been prescribed by a doctor, and is therefore legal, can be misconstrued as being more 'acceptable' to take, than say alcohol or illegal drugs. Don't be fooled my friends, prescription drugs such as OxyContin can carry equally damaging side-effects and addictive qualities as some really hard illegal drugs such as heroin. Sobering stuff.

In a lot of cases it is discovered that a person taking prescription drugs is suffering with mental health issues including depression, anxiety, insomnia, etc., and if one pill is taken to ease off or mask a symptom, another is perhaps needed to pep them up again. The more one takes of certain substances, and that includes medication, even the milder stuff, the more our body builds up a tolerance to it, and therefore more is 'needed' to have an adequate, desired effect.

Recognising if you are masking an underlying mental health issue with a pill or potion designed as a physical health remedy, is key in our own self-awareness, and it's super important to seek help from your doctor and a therapist to help you a) manage the medication dependency and b) to treat any underlying causes.

John and his painkillers

A client of mine, John, had a form of agoraphobia for years. Going anywhere of significant distance rendered him, in his words, a 'nervous wreck'. It was the panic of going away and not being able to get home, and the fear of a loved one dying while he was away, which gradually ramped up his levels of anxiety. Now of course, this fear was deep rooted in a scenario, which had happened in his younger years and hadn't been dealt with appropriately, but as time went on, as each need to go away presented itself, say a work trip or a friend's wedding which proved tricky to swerve *all* the time, in the lead up, John would experience crippling stomach aches, painfully loose bowels and migraines.

Each time, he would reach for the medicine cabinet and 'self-medicate' with a few pills here, and a couple of tablets there, to 'treat' the physical discomfort he was feeling. Once the planned trip had been and gone, either he would have forced himself to go, or at other times the anxiety would have been too much, rendering him house bound under the guise of being 'ill', in which case he would miraculously feel better and the stomach aches and migraines all but disappeared.

Pretty soon though, as life threw up more challenges, with more unavoidable reasons to leave his comfort nest of home, this 'routine' began to get out of hand. The initial respite from having achieved the 'dreaded deed' and having gone away began to ebb away, and the aches and pains took over once again. As they continued and took hold physically, the reach for the pills to mask them became daily, and then to the point where the medication cocktail was consumed 'just in case' with no actual thought or reason behind it. The self-medicating, and his reliance on it, had its grip and was out of control.

Fortunately, John sought help for his growing issue, and with the help of his GP and a therapist (me), we managed to assist his coming off the medication, only using painkillers when he genuinely needed them, and instead worked on the underlying deep rooted problem and cause.

Nanny and the curse of the sleeping pills

Another example of how we can easily fall into a trap of self-medicating physical symptoms of anxiety, instead of addressing the actual underlying cause, comes in the form of my beloved grandma who sadly passed away a few years ago. She certainly wouldn't mind me sharing her anecdote – in fact she felt very strongly about elderly people such as herself having to cope with the unexpected onslaught of anxiety and depression in their twilight years, which is often overlooked, and she was very supportive of me sharing her experience when the time was right.

My Nanny was a mentally strong and independent lady. Having suffered with her physical health for a number of years – dodgy hip and mobility – she found herself at the ripe old age of 93 suffering with night terrors and tremors during the evening, which terrified her. The cause I finally deduced was due to one of the many hospital episodes she'd endured where she'd witnessed a fellow elderly patient pass away in the night, and after some time was, in her words, 'carted off in a black zip up bag', to the mortuary, one presumes.

Now, as sad and routine as this one incident was, my grandmother, who certainly made up for what she lacked in physical agility with a razor-sharp wit and a youthful brain, saw and took in every moment of this scene, and it disturbed her more than anyone could truly appreciate. She started to fear being old and immobile, not being physically in control as she struggled to walk, and dying alone in the night.

Once discharged and back in her own home, my Nanny, with this thought firmly embedded, developed severe anxiety and panic attacks which manifested during the night – a time she was now petrified of, having seen a fellow elderly person meet her maker during those lonely early hours. Now of course, some form of undiagnosed PTSD perhaps was present here which needed treating, and between us we got to the root cause and worked through it to minimise the anxiety. But before we'd got to this ground-breaking moment, my grandmother had been prescribed an impressively worrying amount of medication to help combat the physical symptoms she was experiencing, a lot of it passed off as 'old age', and these included sleeping pills, beta blockers ... I can't even remember some of the meds, but there were umpteen! Of course she was properly medically supervised and cared for, but she did not like the amount of pills she was taking for her various other conditions too.

The dependency on the medication became a cycle of frustration and the grogginess and side-effects the next day were more than a little upsetting for her to deal with. Many people also use sleeping pills more and more in order to combat anxiety, and this is an area which should be carefully monitored if you, or someone you know, is partial to a little medicinal 'help' to aid sleep.

For my beloved Nanny, a relatively straightforward case of anxiety due to a distressing scenario, presented itself as a very physical feeling and experience, and was masked with a well-meant pill to combat it, where in the end, a good midnight chat and reassurance worked wonders. Can you see how a physical symptom can sometimes be so closely linked and exacerbated by an underlying mental health issue? Isn't it a sobering thought that if we are relying on seemingly 'normal' and 'harmless' ways of coping each day, such as painkillers and sleeping pills, that we might actually be self-medicating?

The next exercise is one that I used to do with my Nanny if she needed it of an evening when the physical symptoms, which included chest tightening and the shakes, struck.

My story

Throughout this book I've been honest and open regarding my own experiences of coping with an anxiety disorder, after all, the more we can all understand about mental health, the better, and this chapter on aches, pains and the physical stuff is no exception. I felt it an important inclusion in this guide, as my experiences with the actual physical feelings of anxiety and stress, with hindsight, were such a clue to what I was going through, and I only wish I'd been more knowledgeable back then.

I'm a massive believer in prevention over cure (where possible of course), and early intervention really can serve as a game changer. If I'd known the physical aches and pains I was experiencing on a day-to-day basis were so intrinsically linked to my mental health state, I *know* I would have been better equipped to seek the right support earlier ... who knows, maybe I'd have not developed some of the other symptoms down the line if I'd known? In a weird way, I'm glad I did though so I've been able to share with you from both a personal and professional viewpoint, everything I went through. You can tell I'm a 'glass half full' person!

So what was I going through? Similar to some of the examples I've previously explained, due to the initial whopping panic attack (my particular traumatic event – the 'trigger'), as well as the daily fear and dread, I subsequently began to have some very physical feelings too. Each morning my bowels would be doing a right royal rhumba.

▶

Activity alert

Fans of yoga might be familiar with this approach to total mind and body relaxation. It's such a simple, yet effective, way to significantly reduce feelings of physical tension and pain. Remember, you are in control, and any physical feelings of discomfort, which stem from a mental or emotional trigger, can be 'controlled' by you. Feeling empowered? You should be, you've totally got this! You may like to record this and play it back to yourself, or have a friend take you through it step by step to heighten the experience.

Get yourself in as comfy a position as you can. Lying down is preferable, or you can sit if this isn't possible. Make yourself as comfortable as possible ◌ Be mindful of any background noise ... notice it if it's there and if you're unable to change it, accept it calmly. If you can get into a peaceful room with perhaps some chilled music, then even better. ◌ Remind yourself that you are safe, that you are in control, and absorb yourself with what makes you feel safe, i.e., remind yourself that you have loving family nearby or just a phone call away, or your doctor is easily reached, or you have neighbours simply next door should you need them. Allow this feeling of safety to be fully realised. ◌ Bit by bit, limb by limb, we're going to calmly take our attention to our body and relax each part in turn. ◌ Firstly, take a nice slow deep breath in through your nose, filling your lungs, and then exhale slowly. Do this a good few times to really kickstart the relaxation process – breathing properly is a natural tension reliever. ◌ Start with the top of your head. Notice how heavy and weighty it feels the more you relax it. As you continue the slow breathing, with each breath, allow your head to get even lazier, and even heavier, so that all signs of tension have evaporated. ◌ Next, take your attention to your neck and shoulders, breathing slowly and deeply still, notice how with each breath your neck and shoulders release any tension they might be holding on to. ◌ Repeat this 'body scan', moving down your body from the top and noticing, relaxing and releasing any tension. From the head, neck and shoulders, pause on each body part as you continue ... the trunk/torso, your tummy, then your arms, hands and fingers,

▶

then to your lower back and bottom, moving down to your thighs, calves, feet and toes... ☉ Wiggling each body part gently (where doable) to 'check' that the tension as gone, is a great way to ensure that you have allowed the full relaxation to take place. ☉ Once you have gone through the whole of your body, from top to toe, allow yourself to just lie/sit there for a few moments more, to just 'be'. Notice how relaxed you feel and enjoy the feeling that you CAN lessen the physical symptoms you were carrying a few minutes before. Brilliant empowering evidence that you have totally got a grip on anxiety – not the other way round. ☉ **Well done!**

The accompanying gripey abdomen pains were *seriously* un-fun, and I struggled to control the involuntary 'toilet bouts'. This was particularly embarrassing while having to hold it together (and in!) during a lengthy morning script meeting at Telly Towers.

The headaches, neck strain and tension were a near enough permanent fixture. They never went away. It's a worry when a searing head pain, and crippled shoulders becomes the norm. Now, as a young teen, I was diagnosed with migraines and tension headaches by some hotshot professor in 'the big smoke', and although these had gradually disappeared as I'd gone through puberty, I just assumed somehow they had come back. And this is the worry isn't it, unless you're a raging hypochondriac, the assumption and self-diagnosis can often be *'oh it's just that again'*, or *'I'm not ILL ill'*, or *'a couple of paracetamol will sort it out'*, whereas it could be something more.

I didn't bother to mention these seemingly irrelevant physical issues to anyone, thinking I was just suffering from pre-show nerves (the toilet issues!) and a recurrent headache diagnosis, which I could perhaps treat like I'd done in the past, i.e. a painkiller. What I didn't even give a thought to was that it might be linked to the anxiety, stress and panic attacks that I was experiencing, and had been desperately trying to stave off.

I of course had a few clues, I just didn't open myself up to them at the time, too consumed with trying to 'cope'. If I took myself off to my local Thai massage therapist for a good head and shoulder pummelling, phone turned off, the tranquil panpipe soundtrack soothing my ears, I'd emerge feeling ten times more 'me', with a rare sense of lightness, freedom, and crucially pain free. It of course was a temporary mask, and only took a day for the good work to undo, and for the daily dread, anxiety and stress to get its grip once again, firmly reinstating the headache, neck pain and stomach upset.

Even now, and I profess to 'know better' about myself, if I have a particularly difficult time and I perhaps forget to stick to the 'anxiety busting' principles I know and love (I'm only human after all), as well as the anxiety flutters in my chest and feeling of being overwhelmed, I can feel the familiar twinge of strain and pain in my neck and head, and my bowels will give me a timely reminder that I need to CHILL. It's the physical alarm call I need to help readdress my mental and emotional state – it all works as one big 'team'.

Let's get some self-awareness going on, shall we? The next activity I find really useful when I need to take stock of how my mind and body are working as one, and preventing, or addressing, any unhelpful mental and physical symptoms.

Prevention and early intervention

As I've said before, I'm a big believer in getting 'in there' quick smart to address any niggles, aches and pains as a result of feeling anxious and stressed, *before* they become something more difficult to handle.

I'll be going more in depth into ways we can take care of ourselves in the next two chapters, but to round off this chapter I wanted to share a few tried-and-tested ideas with you which can really help in reducing physical symptoms that might rear up at any time.

I've tried them all and there is certainly something for everyone. Always consult your doctor before undertaking any therapy, and to just rule out anything more troublesome.

- Massage – I can't recommend this enough. Whether it's in the form of sports, Thai or Swedish, a massage is a superb way to work out some of that physical tension and the aches and pains to the body it can cause.
- Acupuncture – not for everybody, not everyone is comfortable with needles, but I find this holistic treatment terrific at unblocking stress and anxiety, and reducing the physical stress.
- Reflexology – a lovely relaxing massage type treatment on the feet. Stress and anxiety can be detected in the body by certain corresponding pressure points on the feet, and then subsequently treated.
- Reiki – a spiritual healing technique, non-body contact, which uses heat and energy from the therapist to identify 'hot spots' of concern on the body, and consequently 'works them out' to a more balanced state.

Activity alert

This exercise is a great reminder that our physiology (our body language) says a lot about us. If we're sitting upright, shoulders back, with a smile plastered across our face, it's more likely we're able to feel happier, positive and more in control. If, however, we sit hunched over, frowning and studying our bootstraps, it's more likely we'll be feeling down and lacking in confidence or motivation.

How we 'hold' ourselves and construct our physiology, can help with feeling more relaxed and reducing any unpleasant physical symptoms, and we can change our internal feelings to match. The outcome – a more relaxed, balanced and physically and mentally healthy you.

First, get creative and choose the 'state' you'd like to be, i.e., confident, relaxed, calm, care-free, etc. ☉ As you identify that new state, really allow yourself to start to notice the feelings and behaviours associated with that. For example, if you choose 'relaxed', you might suddenly and subconsciously take a nice deep breath, roll your shoulders back and sit back in your chair. ☉ In your mind's eye, put yourself in a scenario where you can practise this new state even more. Using your creative mind (you may like to close your eyes to help you concentrate more), visualise where this might be. Perhaps it's your living room, or a cosy kitchen, or a sun lounger on a beach ... really start to allow your imagination to take you where you want, to make the visualisation as strong as possible, and imagine yourself in the picture. ☉ I'm going to ask you to 'dissociate' – which means float out of yourself to a different vantage point in the scene – and look back at yourself in this scenario, and with the new state being experienced and created, keep tweaking how the 'new' you looks and is physically ... are you smiling, is your head up high, are you lying down chilling, are your eyes closed relaxing in the wind, are your shoulders nice and loose, are your legs crossed or sprawled out...? It's your experience, so make it as fabulous as you can. ☉ Next, let's put some feelings into the scene. To accompany that wonderful physiology of the desired state, let's get some internal feelings to match.

▶

Perhaps you're feeling light and airy in your head and shoulders, and you're feeling relaxed, maybe you're thinking of all the simple things that make you happy, who makes you smile, and how about we put some self-congratulation and gratitude in there too for being wise enough to give yourself some time out. ⊙ Finally, in your mind's eye, I want you to 'associate' (step back into your own shoes and look out through your own eyes), experiencing this wonderful scene first-hand, with all the intensity you can muster. Enjoy the internal feelings of the desired state, and actually act out the physical behaviour too. Make this as good as you can, enjoying all the feelings it's bringing you, breathing nice and deeply, and when you're ready, carry on the rest of your day, embracing this 'new' you.

The outcome of this activity is to create a positive state of change for you in a fairly quick space of time. You can do it quietly at work, at home or even on a train! By recognising that you are going to do something about the way you're feeling physically and mentally, can be hugely helpful in changing it instantly. I use this exercise frequently whenever I feel the signs of stress coming on, and it works every time to 'reset' me to being relaxed and confident.

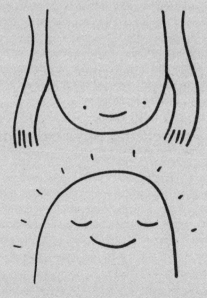

Dr Reetta says...
Aches, pains and the physical stuff

As Anna says, physical and mental health are very much connected. It is now widely recognised that 'mind' and 'body' should not be thought of as separate – having a physical health problem increases the likelihood of having a mental health problem, and vice versa.

When aches and pains are part of your day-to-day life, you probably don't expect to hear that a psychological approach could help. Even if the actual level of pain doesn't change, by examining your thoughts and behaviours in relation to the pain, you can change your response to it and develop new coping methods. Psychological techniques may not take the pain away, but they can help you to feel more in control of your life. You may have developed unhelpful habits or 'vicious cycles', which are easy to get into when you aren't feeling great physically, but aren't the best way to deal with pain.

Anna's 'Activity alerts' in this chapter will help you to deal with the physical sensations by allowing you to relax. As well as reducing anxiety, regularly practising relaxation may reduce pains and aches that are due to tense muscles (headaches, backache, etc.).

Top tips for tackling physical symptoms

Top tip 1

My top tip is to examine what your 'vicious cycles' are. Start by identifying your thoughts, feelings, behaviours and physical sensations in relation to the pain you experience. Then write these down on paper and try drawing some arrows to connect them. For example, if you *think* 'this pain is awful, I can't cope with it', it can lead to you *feeling* depressed, which means you are *doing* less as you are more tired and achy, which

▶

may then lower your pain threshold and leave you experiencing more aches and pains (*physical sensations*). Then, start looking for 'exits' from your 'vicious cycle'.

Top tip 2
Thought challenging can help you find more helpful or realistic ways of thinking about the situation. It may be that the pain you are experiencing isn't going to go away due to a chronic physical health condition – do you think you can learn to live with it?

Top tip 3
Do you need to rethink the balance of activity and rest periods? Aim for a balance of activities that allow you to experience achievement, enjoyment and being with people close to you, as well as resting. Can you do more of the things that help (e.g. increased activity, distraction), and less of the things that make things worse (e.g. thinking and worrying about the pain)?

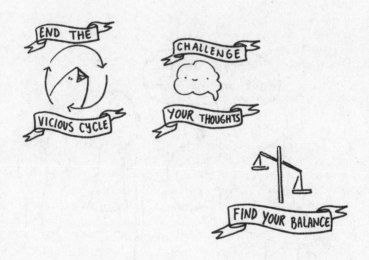

8
DIET, EXERCISE AND APPETITE – THE 'I CAN'T DO THIS' FEELING

Anna's Quick Fix SOS

REMEMBER A HEALTHY BODY AND HEALTHY MIND GO HAND IN HAND You owe it to yourself to give BOTH as much TLC as possible.

PLAN, PLAN, PLAN It may sound dull, but calmly planning ahead as much as you can with your exercise and eating can help get into a healthy routine without it becoming a chore or catching you off guard.

REDUCE ANY STRESS A major 'no' for anxiety anyway, but stress can also affect appetite and motivation. Be your own boss and recognise when you need some chill time.

The antidote of exercise

You may be wondering, what has exercise and eating got to do with anxiety? After all, this isn't a book necessarily designed to preach about squats, lunges and eating lettuce ... however, the correlation between a healthy body and healthy mind has, particularly over recent years, become overwhelmingly established. Later in the chapter I'll be talking all things food, and body and mind 'fuel', but for now, let's shed some light on working up a sweat.

The benefits of exercise for improving physical condition and fighting illness and disease, is well known. It's fairly safe to suggest that most of us, at some point, have been, (or will be) quizzed by a medical professional of some sort about the state of our overall health and how much exercise we do, and how well we're fuelling ourselves with food and water. It might sound monotonous at times, and dare I say it, rather a yawn fest, but, having myself seen the positive impact, I can honestly not place more emphasis on the importance of a decent diet and exercise routine in order to combat and keep anxiety at bay.

Exercise is vital for mental fitness. It can reduce stress and fatigue, and improves our alertness, concentration and brain function. As we know, stress and anxiety are pretty normal parts of our lives, it's knowing how to cope with it that's key, and with stress affecting the nervous system, our hormones (such as cortisol and adrenalin being released), muscle tension which can cause those pesky head and neck aches, and our respiratory system which can make breathing feel laboured as we strive for more oxygen, this subsequently has a direct knock on effect and impact on the body. We can feel lethargic, achy, tense. But, here's the good news, we have the answer sitting inside us all along – when you exercise, endorphins are released – nature's instant feel-good hormone and natural painkiller going to work, helping to decrease stress, tension and anxiety (tick), promote sleep (tick), and boost self-esteem and confidence (major tick).

But what are endorphins *exactly*? You may have heard this word bandied about when it comes to exercise, but many aren't actually too sure what they are, only that people rave about them. Remember, this is a jargon-free book so I promise to keep this as simple as possible.

In our brains we have 'neurotransmitters' which are like little chemical messengers giving off signals to the rest of the body. These neurotransmitters, when triggered by exercise, give off neurochemicals called 'endorphins', and these invisible hormones act as nature's very own painkiller (similar to the pain relief drug, morphine) and bring about feelings of euphoria and general wellbeing – a complementary, and pharmacy visit-free, anxiety and depression buster!

And guess what, the good news keeps coming, there are other 'happy chemicals' that we possess in our clever brains – dopamine, serotonin and oxytocin are also part of the 'feel-good' group.

- **Dopamine** is the 'motivation' chemical, and plays an important role in setting and accomplishing goals, and recognition of achievement. Making sure you celebrate along the way is key to keeping a healthy flow of dopamine going.
- **Serotonin** is the 'self-esteem' chemical, and is boosted when we feel significant, important and valued. Practising gratitude can really

help to trigger this, as can spending time outdoors in the sun so the sun's Vitamin D can give it a boost.

- **Oxytocin** is the 'love' or 'cuddle' chemical and is responsible for intimacy, trust and building healthy relationships. Giving someone a hug can produce this feel-good hormone.

How clever is the human body? Can you see how endorphins in particular are the miracle drug for anxiety? By getting off our butts on a vaguely regular basis, and getting involved in something which increases our heart rate just a smidgeon, we can help bust our anxiety BIG TIME. What have we got to lose?

Now, just to be clear, I'm not suggesting that a diet and exercise overhaul is going to 'cure' any major anxiety you may be experiencing, but in my personal and professional experience, it DOES have a significant impact on your mental wellbeing, and often acting as a welcome distraction from anxiety and stress niggles. I genuinely attribute a physical body makeover, which consisted of starting to exercise (before, I could have been in the running for a couch-potato-of-the-year competition) and making healthier food choices, with significantly reducing my anxiety symptoms, and it's something I make every effort to practise still today. A daily walk outdoors, even for just ten minutes, really helps to boost my mood, focus and relaxation, and I make sure I either get one in first thing in the morning, or before dinner – we can all find ten minutes. I also ensure I eat three meals a day, with some healthy snacks in between, to keep my energy levels flowing nicely. This also gives me a sense of routine and a regular pause of activity, which I find is really helpful in checking in with myself during the day to ensure I'm not letting any stress creep up.

The effect exercise has on our mental wellbeing varies in personal experience and duration, and it can depend on the type of activity chosen, but in general, whether you've had a killer gym session for an hour, or a brisk ten-minute walk, the effects can be just as positive and long lasting. Adopting regular exercise patterns is just good for you – with reduced anxiety, stress and low mood a seriously helpful by-product. In one study, by the Anxiety and Depression Association of America (ADAA), it was suggested that people who take part in regular vigorous exercise, and by that I mean some sort of aerobic or cardiovascular activity which makes you break a sweat, such as running and skipping, were 25 per cent less likely to develop an anxiety or depressive disorder over the next five years.

Getting more active also carries another rather lovely by-product – an improvement in physique and physical appearance, be it weight loss (if needed), less bloating, healthier looking hair and skin, and a more defined body shape ... this in turn will add to your general mojo being boosted, self-esteem soar and an overall feel-good feeling – which is exactly the stuff we need to help keep anxiety at bay.

So far, so good? Excellent. The theory and stats are rather encouraging aren't they? But what about if you just hate the gym, if the thought of donning a pair of trainers and stretchy lycra fills you with dread? Well, fear not, there are many different forms of exercise and activity that can boost, not just your heart rate, but your motivation to want to do it in the first place too. Let's explore, shall we?

Make it a choice, not a chore

I've heard it a gazillion times: *'I want to get up and out there but I just have no energy and motivation'*, and *'that sounds great, but I'm too tired and have no time'* – let's be honest, we've all been there. As we've discovered in the previous chapters, when we're experiencing feelings of anxiety, low mood and stress, all of which are linked to one another, often the last thing we feel like doing is getting trussed up and jumping about like a spaniel on heat, especially if we've also been suffering with sleep deprivation and are feeling like we've been hit by a bus. As I've said throughout this book, I really know how that feels and I understand.

'Readiness for change' is a key part of helping ourselves. I use and explore this notion a lot when I'm working with people who are keen to take control of their anxiety, and who do not want it to overwhelm them anymore. A few years ago, James O. Prochaska, award-winning Professor of Clinical and Health Psychology at the University of Rhode Island, devised a Readiness For Change continuum, which I think makes perfect sense and serves as easy understanding of how we can implement our own readiness for change, and indeed what it might give us in the long run.

In a nutshell, there are five stages of 'change', which we can use as our own checklist for knowing what we want, and how we're prepared to kick it into action. They are:

1   Pre-contemplation – a state of denial, not interested in implementing change, or acknowledging that there may be things that need addressing.
2   Contemplation – unsure or carries mixed feelings about change, but is starting to open up thought processes in the right direction.
3   Preparation – makes a decision, starts to test out small changes and test the water on what change might be like.
4   Action – giving it a go! Making plans and acting them out, and following through with the chosen goal of change.
5   Maintenance – ensuring the goal and motivation is strong enough to continue with the desired change for the foreseeable future.

Understanding where we are in this 5-step plan is really helpful in working out what we want, when we want it, and what ultimately it will give us, i.e., the whole point of doing it. For example, if we are being *really* honest with ourselves, and that's super important – for if we can't be honest with ourselves, who can we be honest with? – and admit that we're perhaps at step 1 (pre-contemplation), where so many of us find ourselves at some point or another in life, and that we actually need to address *that* mindset first in order to be able to shift into the more 'doing' phases of 3 (preparation) and 4 (action).

How can we shift our motivation from '*I can't be bothered*' to '*I can do this*'? By setting a cast iron plan in place, to which we can hold ourselves accountable, that's how.

Finding the right activity

I've briefly mentioned in the activity that follows that finding a sport or hobby that interests you is really important. Be kind to yourself, and ▶

Activity alert

This activity is a little similar to the 'Plan it out, play it out' exercise in Chapter 3. You can re-visit that chapter and borrow the template of the activity, and simply replace the Goal to include smart exercise and food choices.

Have a go at this one too. It's a nice and simple way to channel your perspective and kick start your motivation into action.

CREATE THE GOAL – with the focus on getting active, write down what you're going to achieve (note I've said 'going to', not 'want to' ... we're shifting motivation and readiness for change big time here). Perhaps it's identifying and committing to taking on a new sport or hobby once a week, maybe it's walking the dog at the weekends, or perhaps it's taking the stairs instead of the lift.

ACTION THE GOAL – Give your options and motivation a boost by roping in a friend, signing up online to an activity or course, and give yourself a day and time to get started and write it in your diary/on the kitchen calendar/on your smartphone/on a post it note on the bathroom mirror so you can't miss it, or ignore it! Hold yourself accountable with preparing as much as you can (it's much harder to back out), and organising yourself in advance with whatever you might need, i.e. suitable clothing, transport, refreshments.

N'JOY THE GOAL – finding the right activity for you is crucial and will help you in wanting to go back again and again, and essentially sticking to the goal long term. Explore sports or hobbies you like the look of, are perhaps local to you, and evoke a natural curiosity and desire to give a try (no matter how small the interest at first).

crucially, realistic with what you opt to try. If the most strenuous workout you've taken part in for some time consists largely of opening and closing the microwave oven door, then signing up for a full on marathon might perhaps not be the most realistic, or easy, option at first. It's not to say you can't work up to that, in fact having done it myself, I'd wholeheartedly challenge you to give it a go, but if we're trying to ease ourselves into some nice gentle, anxiety busting exercise, we might be best advised to try something a little less challenging, and ultimately fun, to start with.

Aerobic exercise is championed for its endorphin-releasing qualities, so you might like to have a think about what activities suit and interest you where you can get your heart and breathing working a bit harder than it is when you're slumped on the couch, and work up a bit of a sweat in the process. As always, do consult your doctor or medical professional before you take up a new hobby to get the once over and green light.

Some examples of aerobic exercise to whet your appetite include:

- indoor/outdoor jogging and running
- indoor/outdoor cycling or spinning
- swimming
- walking
- step aerobics
- skipping
- water aerobics
- body pump
- kettlebells
- boxercise
- dance classes such as Zumba, salsa or street dance
- lightweight resistance exercises.

There are other options for getting your endorphin-releasing exercise – these can include joining a club or team sport, which can be a great way to get back into exercise in a social way, and you'll find there are lots of local places giving friendly team sports a push with renewed vigour, you can even play Harry Potter's favourite game, Quidditch! Other sports to try are:

- netball
- football
- tennis
- karate
- 5-a-side football
- volleyball
- basketball
- dodgeball
- squash
- badminton
- hockey
- cricket.

And if you're not quite feeling up to running around like a Duracell Bunny, there are also slightly less strenuous, relaxing forms of aerobic exercise which still carry huge anxiety-busting benefits. These include:

- walking – either a fast-paced power walk or a casual stroll
- yoga
- Pilates
- ballet
- tai chi
- gentle swimming.

The exercises I've outlined are just the tip of the iceberg, to get you started and the ideas flowing. It might be that you try a few to see which ones you like, which ones you wouldn't touch with a bargepole, and which activities ignite an interest – whether you try 1 or 100, it doesn't matter, the point is that you find something you enjoy as you're more likely to stick with it.

Perhaps you fancy yourself as the next Beyoncé with moves to match? Then why not think about joining a local dance class? Maybe you've always wanted to revisit your football-loving youth? Enquire at your local football club, leisure centre or even within your place of work, to see what they offer up by way of amateur teams? Perhaps the thought of rivalling Madonna with her yoga poses excites you? Utilise your website search engine and have a look at which yoga centres are nearby.

Whether it's a casual walk in the garden, a weekly cycle into work, or a full-blown all singing all dancing gym membership, whatever your exercise or activity of choice, the main thing to remember and be proud of, is that you're doing something for you and your health – physical and mental – and you're going a major way to keeping unwanted anxiety and depression at bay to boot. Well done!

My story

You might be forgiven for thinking I'm rather clued up on all this exercise malarkey, and to an extent you'd be right as it's something I've played with and learnt a lot about over the years to alleviate anxiety. I am also now married to a health and fitness professional, who's a personal trainer (handy), who has a terrific understanding of, and approach to, weaving together exercise, diet and mental health. I might have the knowledge and support now, but it hasn't of course always been this way.

Back in 2006, just before 'meltdown day', I was probably what you'd call a 'token gym goer'. I'd dutifully pay my £70 a month membership at a swanky central London gym, and rock up a couple of times a week to have a 'workout'. I say 'workout', as what I did then bears no resemblance whatsoever to what I do now to keep fit – and the irony is I work out for less time for more benefits now, due to a little bit of 'trial and error' and correct guidance.

The old me would faff about in the ladies changing room for far too long getting ready (goodness knows doing what), and then after a gentle trot on the treadmill, a couple of half-hearted sit ups while craning my neck to watch *EastEnders* on the giant TVs, and the obligatory hanging around the water fountain 'killing time', I'd somehow convince myself that I'd done a decent workout, would grab my stuff, and head out of the gym, more often than not straight into a boozy dinner with my mates.

There's nothing inherently unusual, or indeed wrong, about my old habits ... after all, who doesn't behave like this at some point in their 20s, right? But this lack of care for my physical health started to have a gradual, yet direct, impact on my mental health.

These were also the days of long boozy TV exec lunches. It's not quite so the done thing now, but ten years ago a 'lunch' was called at the drop of a hat. 'We've got great viewing figures this week, let's have a lunch!', 'We need an ideas brainstorm session – let's have a lunch!', 'It's so and so's birthday – let's have a lunch!', 'It's Friday – let's have a lunch!'... you get the idea.

As lovely as all these lunches were, they were not without their side-effects. A stodgy meal and glass of vino here and there would leave me feeling sluggish and tired for the afternoon's schedule, which would naturally impact my levels of concentration and lethargy. I only had myself to blame, and no one made me stuff my face with gluttonous food, and to be quite honest with you, I loved it! It was work and play at its best ... working hard and enjoying the downtime with my colleagues with little care for the consequences.

Unfortunately for me, the unhealthy lifestyle I was living physically wasn't doing me any favours in all other areas of my health. The over indulging on calorific meals, combined with the lack of effective exercise, over time began to hinder my motivation, self-esteem and stress levels. As these key elements to my mental health were put under more and more strain, with no adequate outlet for them to be addressed. Throw into the mix a difficult personal relationship and a pressured job role, and BOOM, welcome to 'meltdown day' – the day my panic attacks and anxiety disorder started.

Once I'd seen my doctor and had begun to the get the relevant help and understanding I so desperately needed for my mental and emotional health, the next stop was to have a good look and overhaul of my diet and exercise routines – remember, our mental and physical health is very closely linked.

Step forward my wonderful personal trainer friend Ian Howard, who changed my entire approach to exercise, and the all over mind and body benefits it can bring about. I admit, I was sceptical at first, I mean, *really* how effective was this going to be in curing my anxiety? The answer, it turned out, was very.

Over the following months, regular weekly workouts in the park by ITV Towers not only boosted my mood, self-confidence and gave me an outlet to let out any pent-up stress and anxiety, I also got physically fitter too, which only added to my self-esteem and the happy 'endorphins' which were flowing freely by this point. It's nigh on impossible to feel anxious, stressed and depressed when you're sprinting around a London park in the sunshine working up a sweat – go on, I challenge you, why not give it a try?

Fast forward to present day and arguably I've never looked back. I've always maintained a healthy attitude to exercise, ensuring I plan for it accordingly – a top tip is to prioritise and book it into your diary like you would a really important work meeting or doctor's appointment, so you're less likely to forget – and making sure I do something I enjoy. Whether it's a body pump class, yoga or a jog in the fresh air, I always ensure of a variety to keep me inspired and motivated to stick to it. You'll work out what works for you best, don't be afraid to try a few things out, experiment with the unknown (safely of course), and build some mental health-boosting exercise into your daily life.

You might like to join a local gym, which I've certainly benefited from over time, however, be careful not to sign up for an all singing, all dancing, expensive membership if you're unlikely to use it that often – chances are you'll just feel guilty, which defeats the object of reducing your anxiety. A lot of gyms do taster sessions, or promotions to give you a chance to 'try before you buy', and that's a great way to see if it's for you or not.

You might also like to rope in a friend or loved one, it can be more fun, sociable and motivating to work out together – all good anxiety busters – I often go on walks or a gentle jog with my husband, which is a great way to unwind together, and a natural sleep promoter too.

This next activity can be really helpful at helping you stick to your new fabulous 'active' goals.

▶

Activity alert

Moving away and moving towards

This activity is about developing strong motivations for opposite ends of a 'doing' scale. At one end of the scale we have 'moving away', and the other end we have 'moving towards' – like this:

Away .... Towards

The aim is to build up as strong a motivation as possible 'away' from the old, negative, beliefs and behaviours – in this case around exercise – comprised of feelings, thoughts, pictures, sounds, etc.

In turn, we are going to turn our attention to the other end of the scale and build up a super strong motivation 'towards' where we're heading in terms of our new goals, plans and desired state.

So for example, I want to build up as strong and solid a picture in my mind of the 'old me', how sluggish and ill I felt when I didn't work out properly, how demotivated I felt, how much it impacted my health and emotional wellbeing ... I want to make it as rubbish and awful as possible so I have a really strong desire to get as far 'away' from that as possible, with no intention of going back there. The better the image and thoughts, the more powerful the desire.

In stark contrast, with this 'away' motivation created and parked to one end of the spectrum, I now want to create a really solid and wonderful image of what I'm moving 'towards'. How will it make me feel having a healthy exercise routine? Imagining how brilliant and anxiety-free I will look, feel, and with a big smile on my face perhaps. I want to make this 'towards' image as bright, colourful and aspiring as possible. The better the picture, the more alluring it will be.

Have a go yourself. Experiment with your 'away from' and 'moving towards' images, thoughts and feelings and in particular make that 'towards' being

▶

active motivation as powerful as possible. The more we can make the opposites further and further away from each other, the more we can enjoy sprinting 'towards' a healthier, happier you, and the better the chances of the new behaviour sticking too. The past is the past, let's really focus on creating that fabulous future.

When exercise can be too much of a good thing

So far I've talked about how positive exercise can be on our mind and body, but there are times when exercise can be counterproductive on our health, and this is when it nudges into the area of self-medicating and addiction (see Chapter 6).

It might sound odd that exercise, this wonderful coping method I've been waxing lyrical about, can actually be a negative thing at times, so it's important to be clear about when this applies so we can be assured that our thoughts, feelings and practices around exercise are within healthy parameters.

As I described in previous chapters, people can find themselves on a slippery slope of different ways to 'cope' with anxiety, whether it be drugs, alcohol, gambling, self-harm ... another, perhaps lesser-known, self-medicating practice is exercise. There are several characteristics that differentiate between regular healthy exercise and exercise addiction, which can be counterproductive, and hinder a person's life and health, rather than improving it. These can include being permanently exhausted as a result of working out, giving the body no chance to properly rest and refuel (which can lead to malnutrition), physical injuries, and feeling more stressed and anxious than before as the need to feel the exercise 'high' increases.

Exercise releases endorphins, which, as we know, makes us feel fabulous and energised, and the feel good, 'reward' brain chemical dopamine is also released during regular excessive exercise, which has all the similar characteristics to other forms of self-medicating – it's the pleasurable association, and the sating, feel-good release that can become habitual and a 'need'.

Over exercising can also cause withdrawal symptoms such as feeling low, anxious and irritable, and one can perhaps only feel better once the activity has been commenced again, often with complete disregard to the fatigue and exhaustion the body is already experiencing. As we know, when we neglect one part of our health, the other part will also suffer, so the anxiety and depression we might have been combatting with 'healthy' exercise originally, in all likelihood will do a massive U-turn and continue, or even get worse, as we place stress, tiredness and exhaustion on our mind and body as a result of overdoing it.

People at risk of exercise addiction may be using this excessive behaviour as a way of exerting some control over their lives, where they may be experiencing difficulties. Problems at home, work, relationships, or dealing with inner conflict can all attribute to exercise being the most important thing in their lives, and a way to express any pent-up feelings, or indeed, to block them out.

Just to be clear, exercise is a fantastic way to manage mood, anxiety and stress, but IF the need to exercise becomes greater than your ability to manage your feelings, thoughts and day-to-day life, then it's perhaps a good idea to pop and see your GP or doctor to discuss the situation, and get some further help and advice to learn other ways to cope.

Food, glorious food ... or is it?

So far, we've covered the active side of coping with anxiety, and of course, it stands to reason that if we're jumping and running around boosting our mood and releasing all that pent-up stress, we need to fuel our bodies correctly too. Supporting your physical and mental health with the right food and drink is essential in giving yourself the best foundations for a healthy and happy life.

But when we're feeling a little bit nervous or anxious, we often struggle to eat. It's a common side-effect that I'm sure most people have experienced at some time or another ... in an exam, on your wedding day, before a flight ... the moment stress or anxiety creeps in, our digestive system temporarily shuts down, our saliva dries up, and we feel as though our mouth is full of sandpaper. As we discovered in Chapter 1, anxiety can have a very real physical presence.

When I was in the midst of my panic and anxiety disorder, I couldn't eat properly for weeks, I was just so emotionally stressed ... I'd try, but each time I attempted to put anything down my throat by way of sustenance I physically couldn't swallow it. I'd gag, it felt as though there was a lump in my throat (there wasn't), and no amount of water to aid the lack of saliva would help get it down. My weight rapidly dropped, prompting bittersweet compliments from my friends and colleagues. They didn't realise it, but at the time it was such a backhanded compliment as I knew I was getting thinner (which, after the months of scoffing calorific lunches and dinners wasn't a bad thing), but I also knew it was through the most unhealthy and damaging means, i.e. I was barely eating. I didn't develop an eating disorder per se, as I wasn't trying to control or use food as a coping mechanism, however at the time it was suggested that I was going in that direction. A sobering thought, I can tell you.

There are very real conditions, dysphagia (swallowing problems) and globus pharyngeus (lump in throat sensation) that can be connected to stress and anxiety, both of which, with hindsight, were very apt with me.

Dysphagia can present symptoms such as coughing or choking when eating or drinking, regurgitating food, a sensation that food is 'stuck' in your throat or chest, and excessive drooling of saliva. There can be other, physical health reasons for showing signs of dysphagia, so it's always important to get yourself checked out with your doctor, and there are techniques and advice available to help.

Globus pharyngeus is when a person feels there is an obtrusive lump in their throat, but there is in fact nothing present. It shouldn't affect being able to eat and drink, but can cause unnecessary concern for the sufferer. Stress and tiredness can be a main trigger for globus, so do ensure you get a professional medical opinion and adopt ways to relax and de-stress in order to combat the uncomfortable sensation.

Anxiety and eating disorders

Food can also be used as a form of self-medicating (see Chapter 6). It might sound weird that we can 'medicate' via what we might (or as the case may be, might not) eat and drink, but eating disorders such as anorexia nervosa (limited eating), bulimia (purging after eating) and binge, or comfort, eating (excessive bouts of eating) can sometimes creep in, and is very commonly linked where anxiety is present. As I've said previously, it was suggested by my doctor that I was heading in that rather dangerous direction due to the inability to eat during the height of my panic disorder. Thankfully, it was shortlived as I'd recognised the concern early, learnt relaxation techniques and had support during therapy to conquer the food 'thing' pretty darn quickly.

My issues were primarily physical surrounding the sheer 'blockage' of being able to eat, I *wanted* to eat, however, a lot of anxious people develop the emotional attachments to food and how it can be 'used' to cope. Anxiety often reduces our appetite due to the physiological response to the 'fight, flight or freeze' response (as explained in Chapter 1), however, for some people it's the complete opposite and find they seek comfort in food as a distraction, and as a way to cope with difficult feelings, or as a 'reward' to soothe oneself. It's not necessarily about being hungry, it's the feeling of comfort a full tummy can temporarily offer, to mask pent-up feelings.

Eating disorders often go hand in hand with anxiety and panic disorders, and sufferers can find temporary comfort and pleasure in the control, release and obsessive rituals that come with what we put into (and out) of our bodies. The physical effects and impact of using food as a coping mechanism can be really damaging, particularly if used long term, so it's important to seek help and treatment for *both* the anxiety concerns and the eating issues, if this is something of concern.

Fuel yourself well

Finally, it sounds obvious, but food is good. It's essential for our survival and to help us grow, function and essentially, live. Without good nutrition we would struggle to be the best we can be, and we all deserve the chance to do the absolute best for ourselves, so it makes sense that we should fuel our mind and bodies appropriately.

As well as the obvious physical benefits, there are strong links to nutrition and mental health, with certain foods hailed as 'mental health boosters', which can help combat signs of low mood, depression, and anxiety and stress. There are also foods we should avoid which can exacerbate anxiety.

Foods and drinks to avoid

- Processed 'white' foods such as unrefined flour products – e.g. white bread, white pasta, crisps. These have little nutritional value and cause us to feel sluggish, which doesn't help anxiety as we struggle to get the correct nutrition to boost our mental and physical motivation.
- Fried foods – e.g. fry ups, takeaways. These are difficult to digest and have little nutritional content which just won't help with anxiety and your health overall if your body can't process food properly.
- Refined sugars – e.g. cakes, biscuits, sweets, fizzy drinks. These can act as stimulants and make us feel jittery, and then low once the 'high' has worn off.
- Caffeine and alcohol – coffee, energy drinks, spirits, beer, wine. These stimulants are dehydrating, full of toxins and raise our heart rate, which, after the effects of the 'high' have worn off, can make us feel low, depressed and anxious.

Foods to try

- Wholegrain foods which boost anti-anxiety super mineral magnesium – e.g. wholegrain bran and pasta.
- Omega-3 foods for healthy hearts and brain – e.g. salmon and other oily fish, avocado, eggs.
- Nuts which are high in zinc, in their natural form (i.e. not roasted or processed) – e.g. almonds, walnuts.
- Berries rich in phytonutrients – e.g. blueberries, acai berries.
- Herbal teas – chamomile tea can help in aiding relaxation, and green tea contains an amino acid which can help you to relax and de-stress.
- Lots of water! An effective way to help reduce anxiety and stress levels is to ensure you're not dehydrated.

▶

Activity alert

Tracking your snacking

Keeping an eye on what we're putting into our body is important in making sure we're having enough of the good stuff. We can often conveniently 'forget' what we've eaten, or perhaps what we haven't.

You can use Apps such as My Fitness Pal and The FitDay app to track and journal your daily nutrition. Be careful not to get hung up on the 'dieting' side of things though, this isn't our intention here. Or you can do it the old-fashioned way, which I prefer, and keep a written diary of your nosh.

Get a wall calendar, or chalkboard in the kitchen, or just a good old pen and paper, and jot down the 7 days of the week. ⊙ Split each day into Breakfast, Lunch, Dinner, Snacks and Drinks. ⊙ Either as you go along, or at the end of each day, make a note of everything you've eaten and drunk – and here's the important (and hard) part: *Be brutally honest with yourself!* ⊙ Note the quality and frequency of what you're eating, and make tweaks accordingly to ensure your diet is as balanced and full of the anxiety busting good stuff as possible. ⊙ Once you're into the swing of things, how about starting to plan ahead and jotting food ideas in to the next week's diary template. This is hugely helpful in the right choices becoming the norm, and avoids any last minute panic of 'what do I eat today?' ⊙ You might like to share your food diary with a friend or partner ... increasing motivation and accountability.

Other things to consider:

Herbal supplements and vitamins: These can be an effective way to supplement and boost your mood, nutrition and exercise, but should always be thoroughly researched, explored and consulted with your GP before taking, particularly if you are on other medication. They can also carry differing opinions on effectiveness. Some of my personal favourites for anxiety busting, but shouldn't be read as a recommendation for everyone, include:

o   Magnesium and Epsom salts baths (can help to reduce muscle tension)
o   Vitamin B, which includes B1, B3, B5 and B12 (can help control blood sugar and lactic acid which can contribute to panic attacks, and helps produce serotonin which promotes sleep)
o   Gamma Amino Butyric Acid (GABA) (is believed to protect nerve cells from getting too burned out due to stress as it promotes calm)
o   Inositol (can help produce serotonin which reduces anxiety and stress).

Of course we are all human, and the odd treat here and there is going to happen, and in my opinion should be embraced and celebrated from time to time. Follow the 'everything in moderation' rule: if you ensure you're adopting healthy food and drink choices the majority of the time, you'll be doing the best service to your mind and body, and keeping those anxiety symptoms at bay.

A few of my Top 3 foodie handy hints to get you started

• **Cook in bulk** – buy a big portion of chicken breasts, beef mince or Quorn (or whatever you like), and make a big batch of your favourite healthy meal (there are loads of recipes available at the tap of a button online, or in your favourite cookery book). You can fill up several Tupperware containers, pop in the fridge or freezer, and take one to work each day to stop you trotting to the handy chip shop, or have one for dinner when you get home – this will help you if you're prone to stray to the takeaway when life gets a bit busy.

- **Carry healthy snacks** – we all get caught out with a hunger pang from time to time, avoid reaching for a sugary chocolate bar from the vending machine, which will give you a temporary 'energy high', but then followed by the obligatory low mood crash, and instead prepare yourself each morning with a handy bag or box of nutritious, slow release energy snacks, such as, grapes, hummus and carrot sticks, homemade flapjack or granola bars, a banana, or oatcakes.

- **Water, water everywhere, so have a drop to drink** – staying hydrated really helps in warding off anxiety, often those who are feeling anxious are dehydrated too. Keep a bottle of water with you at all times and get into a habit of drinking from it regularly. We should be aiming for around two litres of water a day.

Dr Reetta says...
Diet, exercise and appetite

It can feel like life is full of decisions and dilemmas about how to achieve good health. Whether it is about eating the right foods, doing enough exercise, or maintaining your achieved goals around diet and exercise – there is so much information out there. Some of it is conflicting, some of it is confusing, so it can mean it is difficult to make decisions about what's best for you. Making those decisions, finding the motivation and then maintaining lifestyle changes can become a very tricky process, and it's unfortunately easy to lapse out of good habits without much thought. Many people have a cycle of creating good and then lapsing into bad habits throughout their lives. Especially because this process almost always involves issues around confidence, self-image and self-respect. Have a think, could working on one of the above issues be a key to getting yourself to address your diet and exercise goals? Could you, for example, speak more encouragingly to yourself, rather than criticising yourself?

Anna talked about the concept 'readiness for change', which is useful in assessing when to embark on a change of lifestyle. Once you are 'ready', keep an eye on your attitude. To increase your belief in yourself as someone who can make changes, you need to experience success, and to do so, your goals need to be specific and achievable. Have a think about suitable rewards to keep you going on working on your goals.

Top tips for tackling your diet and exercise

Top tip 1
Anna's Activity alert 'Tracking your snacking' will help you understand the patterns you have developed. My top tip involves adding another layer to this 'food diary' by including comments about your mood – this will

▶

give you an insight into any links between foods you eat and emotions you feel. You will most likely notice patterns around moods influencing what you eat, and vice versa, foods triggering certain emotions.

Top tip 2
Another tip is to do with the decisions about what to eat. Rather than banning or limiting foods, have a think about what (something healthy) you can add to your diet.

Top tip 3
The exercise mood boost is a well-researched fact, and most people know that they feel good after exercising. What people often struggle with is how to find the time and the motivation to exercise, as well as how to break the habit of whatever you are doing at the times when you could be exercising. Your habit might be sitting on the sofa in the evenings, watching TV, or comfort eating unhealthy food (or both!). Once you have identified your habit and decided you want to change it, replace it with an alternative behaviour (e.g. exercise, healthy snacks). If you persist and do this consistently, over a period of time, you will soon have created another, more positive, habit.

9

TALKING, SHARING AND CARING – THE *'FEELING BETTER'* FEELING

ONE BOTTLE OF

FEELINGS

WARNING: CONTENTS UNDER PRESSURE MAY BURST!

Anna's Quick Fix SOS

TELL SOMEONE HOW YOU FEEL Bottling feelings and issues up will only build up and eventually spill over. Identify someone you trust to talk to.

WRITE IT DOWN Talking is fabulous, but if you find it difficult at first, write down how you're feeling and either keep it just for you, or share it with someone you feel able to confide in.

EMPATHISE WITH OTHERS As we know, there are millions of other people also feeling how you might be at some time in life – letting others know you understand can do wonders for your own mental health and feeling of wellbeing.

A problem shared

I'm sure you've heard the old saying, 'a problem shared is a problem halved' – *discuss your problems with someone, and then there are two of you considering a possible solution.* I love this definition, and it's certainly one very possible outcome, the act of sharing your feelings with someone, of talking and offloading can do wonders for unburdening yourself and just getting the pressure, or niggles, or worries out of your head and into the open – preferably in a safe and confidential place.

Talking – it sounds easy enough, doesn't it? But let's be honest, how many times in life have you had a niggle or annoyance with something or somebody, with a cry for help or frustration on the tip of your tongue, only for you to feel stuck for words and unable to spit it out and get it off your chest? It's a normal and natural reaction. But it can leave us feeling frustrated, annoyed, worried and as though we haven't 'dealt' with it. Why do we seem to have this 'block' when it comes to saying something?

Well, we're often apprehensive about the reaction we might get, which is perfectly understandable. The 'right' words can be hard to find and put together at times, especially if we're not used to talking openly and honestly.

Hindsight is a wonderful thing and it's easy to feel irritated if a situation has been left unresolved, with resentful feelings of not being heard festering away. If this has happened to you, as it has to me many times, it can feel as though a 'weight' is being carried. If these feelings are left to fester and build like a pressure cooker, with no outlet to let off steam, mark my words, it *will* come out somehow, and more often than not it can be the simplest, most trivial of triggers that sparks what my husband calls a 'gorilla moment' – angry, yelling, King Kong-like stomping around.

A similar pattern of behaviour applies to other areas of our life, not just when we're annoyed, and none more so than when we're faced with talking about our feelings, our innermost private thoughts. Somehow, the very act of communicating what we're *really* thinking and feeling can feel like the hardest task. I can understand that. After all, what we keep inside our heads is fiercely unique, private and provides us with a level of security. Getting it 'out' can feel incredibly scary and naturally induce feelings of vulnerability, as we can never be 100 per cent sure about how it will be received.

We worry about not being taken seriously, as though we should just 'get on with it and stop moaning', of being seen as 'mad' or a 'weirdo', or that somehow we are burdening people with our worries. It can feel daunting to open up to family and mates for fear of no longer being seen as 'fun' and a laugh, and instead suddenly being labelled 'boring', 'troubled' or 'odd'.

This is where I hope to relieve some of that worry and anxiety. My own personal experiences, and the ones I have on a daily basis with my clients and social media followers, have proven that unlocking that communicating skill (and it *is* a skill, which I'm going to help you hone and finely tune) and confidence, in order to explain and share what's going on in our lives, can be highly effective, and indeed the ultimate piece in the jigsaw puzzle, in getting help and support for anxiety and all your mental health needs.

Who can I talk to?

At this stage I just want to be clear about what I mean by the act of 'talking'. I have taken the liberty of making the assumption that you are able to physically talk, but I know only too well that this isn't always possible for some. So for purpose of clarity, and so we're all on the same page, when I refer to 'talking', what I mean is your chosen way to 'communicate' by whatever method you are able, i.e. writing or drawing, as well as the literal act of speaking.

Identifying the *right* person to talk, or communicate with, is pretty key. Who can you think of in your life who you trust? Do you have a partner, or a family member who has a sympathetic ear? Maybe a good friend or colleague could be an empathic listener? It might even be your personal trainer or friendly neighbour? If you really can't think of anyone in your close circle, despair not, there are plenty of other options to consider.

Your GP or medical professional is a good place to start, but it's worth doing some research into how appropriate for you they are. I know only too well that when it comes to matters of mental health it's so important you see someone who has the appropriate bedside manner, training, time and understanding. You are in all likelihood, going to be unloading your innermost feelings, which can be a big deal, and it's super important you feel as comfortable and respected as possible.

I'm not for one minute knocking doctors, far from it, they have literally saved my life, and I have many wonderful talented friends who work in this field and who are deeply passionate about their work and patients. But I've also heard first-hand stories of people, having geared themselves up with all the courage in the world to finally ask for help, only to be whisked in and out of an eight-minute doctor's appointment having felt very shortchanged with the time, empathy and guidance they were so desperately seeking – often it can take that long just to find the right words.

We are so fortunate in the UK to have a National Health Service, and I'm fiercely proud of it. But I have also seen and heard too many times for comfort over the years, of anxiety and depression sufferers not being given the time and attention they need in order to get the appropriate help. In defence of doctors and surgeries, their time is limited, with many patients to deal with, and I fully appreciate that tight schedules are a fundamental part of running a functioning system. It's a catch-22 it seems.

So, what can you do about it? Despite any of the above challenges, I still strongly always recommend your GP as your first port of call. They are in a fabulous resourceful position to refer anyone in need on to other services and help should it be required. Talking therapies such as counselling and CBT are now available on the NHS, albeit you might have to wait your turn, and waiting lists can be long. GPs can also administer and monitor appropriate anxiety medication should it be appropriate – which I chat about in previous chapters.

In order to give ourselves the best help we can, it's worth doing a little research, and some prep work, before you go to see your GP. Most doctors work out of a surgery, often alongside several other doctors and medical professionals. Find your local GP surgery and start by making a telephone call to the reception. You can always ask to speak to the Practice Manager too, and in confidence, ask them if they can recommend the most appropriate GP within the practice who is trained and empathetic in mental health matters. You can then request to see them specifically.

Until very recently, mental health training for GPs in the UK wasn't mandatory, and it has certainly been reflected in the cases I hear of a 'pot luck' gamble as to whether you get an understanding GP. And it really can make ALL the difference in terms of where you turn to next.

One client of mine eventually came to me for help after being put off by an experience he'd had with his GP. After months of suffering with panic attacks, he finally got the courage to make an appointment and disclose his innermost thoughts and feelings regarding his mounting anxiety and depression. He'd barely opened his mouth to bravely ask for help, when he was brusquely told by the doctor that he 'hadn't got enough time to deal with this', and to 'come back another week and make a double appointment instead'.

My client was so dejected and put off by the seeming 'brush off', that he reverted back to his 'pit of despair' for another SIX MONTHS, feeling embarrassed and a time waster. He was of course nothing of the sort, and I'm sure the doctor didn't mean to imply that he was, however, goodness knows how different his experience might have been had he been met with a sympathetic ear instead.

Fortunately, the medical profession is realising how vital mental health training is, and it is now something which is growing as an essential part of mandatory, and essential, medical training ... in this case, it isn't too little too late ... it's better late than never!

Who else can I talk to?

Of course you don't *have* to go to your GP for help. You might like to have a think about alternative people and places to get the appropriate support.

Starting with a good friend or trusted family member is often a great way to start talking, and crucially be listened to in confidence. The support and empathy they can hopefully offer can then spur and encourage you to seek more tailored, professional help, if required. I find that taking your confidante along to your first appointment, even if they just wait in the car or in the waiting room for moral support, can be really comforting.

Talking therapies, which include counselling, psychotherapy, psychiatry, CBT, Neuro Linguistic Programming (NLP), hypnotherapy, and mindfulness, among others, are all services that can be found and undertaken privately (a little breakdown of these therapies is on pages ix–xi). Some people actually prefer this way of getting help, as there is less 'paper trail' of being in a system, should they wish to stay anonymous, and they can feel more in control of what intervention they choose – there is a price to pay though, literally.

Some therapies are available on the NHS (which is great), but often due to increasing need and overwhelming demand on stretched services, waiting lists for appointments can be up to a year in some cases. There is a government initiative called Access and Waiting Times Standards developed in 2014 by the department of health in association with NICE, which aims to ensure that people receive appropriate mental health care and at least a follow-up appointment with a mental health professional within 6 weeks of having seen their GP and being referred. So this will hopefully make a difference for waiting times from now on, and the potential wait should not be something that puts you off seeking help.

As a result of long waiting times, more people are turning to self-funded private care, which tends to be more instantly accessible but can cost anything from £25 to £150 a session and perhaps, depending on the therapist, even more. Of course the NHS is not a bottomless pit. In an ideal world there would be instant, free access to services. Anyone who campaigns for mental health awareness believes that early intervention is vital, but until that time comes, we have to do the best for ourselves with the resources on offer.

Tools such as this book, accessing charities for support such as Mind (www.mind.org.uk), and looking into a private therapist are all available to you at the click of a button. Websites such as www.thencp.org, www.counselling-directory.org.uk and www.bacp.co.uk can all point you in the right direction to find a qualified and accredited therapist suitable for your needs, your postcode, and your pocket.

Anyone can see a counsellor, coach or therapist, it doesn't matter what your gender, race or religion is, there is help out there for you should you choose to ask for it. A benefit of seeing a trained professional, whether on the NHS or privately funded, is that they (and, as a therapist, I put myself into this professional category) are virtual strangers to the client. This is often an attractive choice, and preferable to talking to a friend or family member exclusively, as there is no emotional attachment. Therapists are trained to listen, in confidence, and not judge, with the sole aim of helping unburden the person seeking help. A talking therapy session can help you find your own answers, in your own time, with an opportunity to look at your problems in a different way, in surroundings which are fully respectful of you and your opinions.

Often it's a chance to cry, shout, talk, laugh, or just think in your own space, and it never fails to amaze me how valuable this time and space can be for individuals needing to make sense of their situation and feelings. Some people say that talking therapies don't make their problems go away, but they find it easier to cope with them and feel

just let it out

AHHHHHHH

there you go!

happier... and when we feel happier, feelings of anxiety are more likely to dissipate.

Visiting a therapist – what to expect

Making the appointment to see a therapist, coach or counsellor can be daunting enough, let alone the actual first session. Many people are nervous and apprehensive about their first session – it's completely normal, after all you're going to be talking about your innermost thoughts and feelings! I'd go as far as to say that EVERY client I work with is nervous at their first session, it's something therapists are very used to, they should make every effort to help you feel at ease, and I bet you'll feel so much less worried by the time you finish.

Choosing your therapist

Websites such as the ones I've mentioned previously are a great place to start if you're unsure of what kind of therapy or therapist you'd like. Whether it be a counsellor, life coach or psychologist, check what qualifications they have, how long they've trained and been practising, and whether they are a member of a professional body such as the ones I've listed.

It is also worth asking if they have training and experience of working in your particular area of concern. A good therapist should always recommend someone else, perhaps better suited to your needs, if they feel it's not their area of expertise.

Choosing your method

There are various ways in which to have a therapy session, the internet has transformed the traditional face-to-face in person appointment, which is still the most practised method, but you can now opt to have one-to-one therapy via the internet (Skype, FaceTime, Webinar), telephone and email too.

Cost, time and travelling are all factors to consider when choosing how and where you'd like your session, and the choice can really open up your options to ensuring you get the therapist best suited to you and your needs, in the communication style you prefer. I have a client based in the northern part of Scotland where he says therapy resources for him are limited, as well as his time, due to family commitments. Thanks to the internet, we've been able to have effective weekly sessions via Skype, where he has seen great progress and change – all in the comfort of his own home.

Have a think about what type of session appeals to you, and why.

The first session

The first appointment tends to last longer than subsequent sessions, normally around an hour and half (follow-up sessions will be around 50–60 minutes in duration) and serves to be an introductory, getting to know each other, ice breaker.

The therapist will take you through their confidentiality policies, and ensure you feel safe and secure in the environment you've chosen to be in. It's a chance for you to ask questions (you might like to have jotted some down prior to the session to ask), for your therapist to ask you several things too, such as, what has brought you to therapy? What would you like to achieve? What are your symptoms? As well as explaining to you how they work: what ideas and approach they have, timescales, and agreeing a plan going forwards together.

Follow-up sessions

You and your therapist will work out how many sessions you mutually feel is appropriate and doable. Most sessions will last for up to an hour, as this is considered the optimum time for concentration – for both client and therapist. You may or may not be set tasks, or homework, which some people enjoy as a way of continuing the good work of the session, and some like to be held accountable to their therapist in this way too, to ensure they're progressing.

Ending therapy sessions

Deciding when to break, or finish, therapy sessions will be something your therapist will chat to you about, and monitor throughout your sessions. Some people only have the one session, others go on to have a set programme, and it can also be something open-ended on an ad hoc basis. Speak to your therapist about your sessions, and ensure you're fully aware and happy with what is suggested and agreed.

Self-harm and the positive effect of talking

In previous chapters we've explored self-medicating and other, harmful ways of coping. Self-harm is also something that creeps into this category and is often used as a coping mechanism for dealing with pent-up feelings. Talking, and therapy sessions, are particularly useful and cathartic for people who self-harm as a way of getting the feelings 'out' in a much safer and healthier way.

If we feel unable to express ourselves verbally or communicate in other ways such as writing things down, a worryingly growing proportion of people (and it's not just teens as some might think) turn to hurting themselves as a way of releasing unexpressed inner pain. Recent figures released by the NHS (from a survey in 2014) suggest that up to a quarter of young women aged 16–24 are self-harming. Self-harm is where someone wants to purposefully harm themselves, and can include cutting to induce bleeding, hair pulling, hitting or punching self, scratching or pinching, carving (such as symbols or words into the skin), and burning.

It's important not to judge anyone who's self-harming, and instead to be empathetic and accept that this person would benefit from learning another outlet for their pain, control and frustration. Talking is a natural go-to but can take a lot of people time and patience to try. If you or someone you know is self-harming, do consider a trip to your GP for help and support. You could also have a look at www.selfharm.co.uk or www.mind.org.uk for lots of information and advice. The main thing to remember, you're not alone and there IS help out there.

Talking and communicating, as we've mused over, can be a really tough and an alien situation to find ourselves in. But with the benefits far outweighing the negatives, it's perhaps worth summoning up all those skills I *know* you have bubbling away inside you, and taking a tentative step into the world of talking about *you*.

My story

Those who know me, know that I can talk ... a lot. In fact one of the first things my late father-in-law said to me in his heavy Italian accent was, *'Anna, you talk too much!'* – some lasting impression I made! I guess as a TV and radio presenter for the past umpteen years, being comfortable and skilled in talking the hind legs off a donkey, or 'filling' as we call it, is a key skill, it's kind of par for the course and it's what I enjoy. But it's one thing chatting to viewers, listeners and reciting a script, and another talking about my innermost thoughts and feelings. In fact it's a whole new ball game, and one that took me several years to master and be comfortable with.

I always *thought* I was a good communicator, and I suppose in the main, when it came to work in particular, I was. However after 'meltdown day' it became blindingly apparent that I was utterly atrocious at talking about the 'other' part of me, the real me, the part that made up my daily niggles, opinions and feelings, the part that no one else could see or hear – the loud, unspoken inner thoughts and words that reverberated around my overflowing head with no outlet to release them. Now, of course there was an outlet, in the form of my therapist. I had to actually *let* them out, but I didn't know how.

The tricky relationship I was in had unwittingly conditioned me to keep quiet and just 'get on with it' for fear of making a fuss, burying any upset or confusion deep within, hoping it would just go away. I was a master of proclaiming to be 'fine', if people asked after my wellbeing, when I was feeling anything but at the time. Yet for so long something stopped me from just blurting out, *'I'm not ok, HELP'*. So what WAS stopping me...? Fear, that's what. Fear of embarrassment and fear of the unknown, of opening a can of worms to try and make sense of the horrible unexplained anxious feelings. And yet, the moment I *finally* cracked and uttered the word, *'help'* ... the load lightened immediately.

▶

Activity alert

The brain dump

Getting our feelings 'out' is often the first step to seeking help and support. Easier said than done though, right? *What* do I say? *How* do I say it? *When* do I say it? These are the questions we find ourselves mulling over when it comes to communicating effectively.

Here are a few tips, which I find really useful when it comes to telling those trusted others, how you're feeling.

Choose your medium. Perhaps it's pen and paper, a smartphone or tablet, it might be a spidergram, mindmap or brainstorm chart (see examples below), or maybe a letter to either your trusted confidante, or even to yourself. Whatever your way to get your feelings and anxieties out, choose whatever feels right for you and GO FOR IT ... I like to call it the Brain Dump because we're going to do exactly that – dump all your thoughts, feelings and anxieties. ☉ Be honest with yourself. This can be the hardest part. When we're holding nothing back, there is nothing left to niggle or hide away inside our head. Allow yourself to feel liberated as you jot down everything you're feeling and experiencing. Remember, these are your private innermost thoughts and feelings, and you have full control over who you choose, if anyone, to share them with. ☉ Be creative. Sometimes we can identify with the words in a particular song, or story or poem. It can be therapeutic and helpful to utilise and absorb someone else's words which perhaps reflect your own feelings. ☉ Share it. You might like to keep your wonderful work to yourself to re-read when you need to (it can be helpful and enlightening to see it staring back at you), or you might find it liberating to burn or throw away the piece of paper ceremoniously as you 'throw out the feelings'. Or you might choose to share your Brain Dump with another. A trusted friend, or family member, or even take it with you for your GP or therapist to read. ☉ Choose your moment. If you choose to share your Brain Dump, good for you! Have a think about picking the right time and place to communicate with your trusted person. Make sure they're not busy or distracted, that they are feeling relaxed and have time to listen, and prepare them by laying the foundations in advance asking them for some time, whenever is convenient, for you to have a chat. Note your body language and tone of voice (if you want to speak), and prepare yourself for the occasion so you feel as comfortable and in control as possible.

From personal experience, I totally get the notion of hitting rock bottom before you can work your way back up, and after being sent home and signed off 'sick' for a few weeks, I finally accepted that I needed to confide in those nearest and dearest around me. I pretty much had no choice, as everyone was naturally concerned about why I was off work and living back at home with my parents temporarily, during what was the busiest month in television.

I started by being honest with myself. I had to trust those around me, the people who knew me the best, to listen, accept and support how I was feeling. My parents, who are my rocks, were just incredible in every way I could hope for. Until that point, I hadn't wanted to worry them – I know a lot of people feel the same – but it was a fruitless exercise as they had been beside themselves for months anyway knowing something was wrong, but feeling helpless and completely in the dark.

My brothers also proved to be a crucial part of my support network. Not ones for talking about their own feelings, it was what they 'didn't' say that helped. No mickey taking (for once), a cup of tea given when needed, and I seem to remember my younger brother James and I had a movie marathon together one night, both sitting in a content silence of companionship – a memory which always leaves me feeling grateful for the simple security it offered. They just knew that Sis wasn't having a good time and I am grateful always to them for just being there for me, and giving me that safe space I needed.

Friends also played a huge part in me getting better. I didn't have a decent excuse any more. I'd become adept at hiding my true feelings, pretending I had a migraine or something equally believable (I hoped) if I wasn't feeling up to a night out due to anxiety issues for instance. I *finally* let them in, and talked to those closest to me. I only wish I'd known then what I know now, and that is to trust in those that were (and are) always there for me, and not to be embarrassed. They're all a great bunch, the very best in fact, each and every one of my mates was there for me with an open ear, shoulder to cry on, and a well-timed brew – and boy, it felt good to talk!

My consultant psychiatrist, Dr Schapira, was also a key person in me getting the help I needed. The chatting to friends and family was helping no end, but there were still some things that I didn't quite know how to articulate or offload. I needed, and wanted, impartial professional help.

I loved the fact that I didn't know him prior to my sessions. He was a stranger with no emotional attachment to me, or opinion, and he didn't know anyone else in my life. This fact was overwhelmingly liberating, and with his expertise, his techniques, which included hypnosis (see below), really helped to tease out the deepest and darkest feelings and fears, which had been buried away. In that little doctor's office, for an hour a week, I would talk, cry, and learn how to offload, as all the pent-up feelings would just tumble out. I also learnt to accept myself, and the situation I had found myself in. With Dr Schapira's help and guidance, I learnt relatively quickly, who I was, and what I needed in order to be a happy human being. Crucially, I also learnt how to control the anxiety and panic attacks.

What is hypnosis?

Hypnosis is the induction of a state of consciousness in which a person is highly responsive to direction or suggestion, and where 'change work' can take place. It is defined as an 'altered state of human consciousness', and is often used as an effective relaxation technique. During a hypnotic 'trance' the client is fully aware and in control at all times, as the practitioner guides and explores thoughts, feelings and memories, with verbal prompts, exploration and cues.

Hypnosis can feel like being in a 'day dream', those in 'trance' are not asleep, in fact they are fully alert and conscious at all times, simply 'tuning out' any unnecessary noise and stimuli to focus on the presenting issue or concern. There are questions over how effective and how much evidence there is to back up how helpful hypnosis can be in treating anxiety disorders, however there are many (including myself) who rave about the pros, and the uninhibited relaxation it can promote. Always choose a qualified hypnotherapist with a solid healthcare background and accreditation.

Values and beliefs

Working on my values and beliefs was a big part of discovering, and accepting who I am. Values and beliefs are at the core of who we are, and make up what is important to us, and they help create a solid foundation for what we stand for in life. Values shouldn't be compromised as they are the fundamental backbone of you, and they can really help in finding clarity, peace and contentment.

When other influences cloud our judgement and perspective, as I found when I was being overwhelmed by feelings of exhausting debilitating anxiety, we can lose sight of what's important to us, and who and what we are. Getting our values and beliefs back in play, and implementing and realising them proudly is a great way to building back up any lacking self-esteem and confidence, which is often common when dealing with the uncertain beast that is anxiety. Let's give it a go, shall we...

Caring is sharing

It might sound a bit woolly, a tad daunting perhaps, but caring about others can be hugely therapeutic for your own 'recovery', a nice little double whammy if you like. You've heard the phrase *'it takes one to know one'*, and in my experience there is no truer place for that saying than when one has been through the journey that anxiety brings.

Demonstrating empathy and sympathy to others will not only be gratefully received, but will do wonders for your own self-esteem and confidence. I can spot someone a mile off who is experiencing a moment of panic or trying to cope with a bout of anxiety. Perhaps before I'd experienced my own situations I wouldn't have had a clue, but once you've been there, you will often notice similar signals in others – and the beauty is, you'll know exactly how to help them by offering a word or gesture of reassurance and understanding.

Questions such as *'are you ok?'*, and *'would you like to talk?'* are so simple, yet so effective.

▶

Activity alert

In this activity I want to tease out those fabulous values (what's important to you), which are unique and special to you. Values are personal and we place them in an order of importance, i.e. how much they mean to us and shape our thoughts, feelings and actions.

> Examples of some popular values are:
> Trust
> Loyalty
> Success/Wealth
> Health
> Communication
> Love
> Security
> Honesty
> Privacy
> Happiness
> Peace
> Confidence
> Integrity
> Work ethic
> Responsibility
> Compassion
> Empathy
> Judgement
> Charity

Have a think about what your values are. Jot them down on a piece of paper and list as many as you can think of and what's important to you. ☉ Now, we're going to narrow them down a tad and create a Top 5 of your most important values. Create a list and decide which of your values should be at No 1, i.e. the most important. Then work your way down the list to No 5, putting your chosen values in order of importance. ☉ **Check in and ask**

▶

yourself, 'if I could have No 1 but not No 2, would that be ok?'... if the answer is 'yes', then that value is in the right place of importance in your Top 5. If however, the answer is 'no', that's a good indication that you might need to shift and play with the order a bit more to ensure it is right. ☺ Keep asking yourself that question as you work your way down, i.e. 'if I could have that higher placed value and not the next one down would that be ok?', until you are satisfied that you have your Top 5 Values in place. To give you a helping hand, as it stands, this is my Top 5 Values:

Anna's Top 5 Values

>   Happiness
>   Security
>   Relationships
>   Communication
>   Trust

Once we have our Top 5 Values in place, and believe me it can chop and change as we start to really work out what we mean by each value we place importance on – this is good and is the point of the exercise – we can then pick a value and brainstorm the Beliefs that surround and support that value. ☺ I enjoy doing this part of the activity by drawing a spider or satellite gram, or you could just create a list. Place your chosen value in the middle of the page, or top of the list (start with your No 1 first as it's the most important), and get creative with 'what needs to happen in order for this value to be met effectively' – this is your 'Belief'. ☺ For example, if we were to take my No 1 Value of 'Happiness', I would jot down my core beliefs of how this value needs to be met and supported like this:

Value = Happiness
Beliefs =

1) spending time with my family and friends

2) taking time for me to relax

3) having a good chat and laugh

▶

(I would then continue to list my beliefs as much as I felt appropriate, and do the same with the other values – it's amazing how interlinked you'll find them all.)

This simple, yet effective activity can be great fun, full of positivity (which is great at diluting any anxiety), hugely empowering, and can really help in reminding yourself who you are, and what's important to you.

Exploring our values in this way can be really eye opening, sometimes surprising, as we discover that what we 'thought' was most important, i.e. responsibility and wealth, actually isn't a patch on how high we might place other values, such as loyalty and communication, and what they 'give' us – which can make all the difference to how we might approach our lives going forwards with more clarity and purpose.

Knowing our values helps us to be more in control of our actions and emotions, recognising what we need to do to feel good, and finding lots of different ways to fulfil them. A hugely positive anxiety-busting exercise – enjoy.

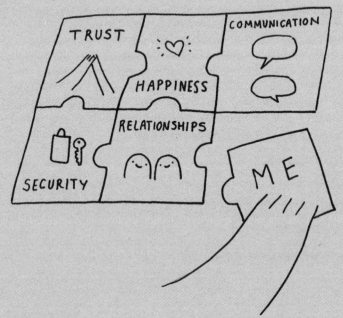

Never underestimate how appreciated it is when you notice others. Take the time to listen to your friends and family in turn, ask them how *they're* feeling from time to time, and let them know you have an open ear should they ever want a chat.

Looking out for others, should we feel up to it of course (got to look after number one first, remember), isn't just a jolly nice thing to do, it's also hugely helpful for that other person who has perhaps been struggling without the skills or tools to get help, and can make all the difference in their lives. It'll also make you feel pretty great to boot. Win win.

Focusing on the future

When we have a clearer idea of where we're heading, why we're heading there, and how we're going to get there, life can feel brighter, liberating, exciting even.

I know from my own experiences over the past ten years or so, that increasing my self-awareness, gaining knowledge about how and why certain things have happened to me, and crucially accepting and understanding my life and working out who I am, has without a doubt, changed my path for the better.

Make no mistake: it hasn't been plain sailing, it wasn't a case of waving a magic wand over my life as it was to miraculously bring about a perfect happy-go-lucky one. There have been hiccups and blips along the way, but ultimately I haven't looked back. That scared, emotionally naïve people-pleaser has moved over as a result of learning from my anxiety and panic disorder.

This might sound odd but I'm actually *thankful* for my yesteryear anxiety, panic attacks and diagnosis, I've made peace with it. Without that major blip in my early twenties, I honestly wouldn't be where, or who, I am today.

And who *is* that, you might ask? Well, I'll leave you to make up your own mind on that one, and hopefully you'll be kind, but from my perspective, I have emerged a happy, content, non-judgemental, empathic, self-aware and much more open and calm person.

▶

To even write those words makes me feel strangely emotional and proud. I'm not 'cured', I don't believe in labelling anyone 'cured' in anxiety circles. That somehow suggests we might never feel that way again, and we know that anxiety is healthy and it is normal ... when used in the right way.

Over the past ten years I have been committed to helping others who feel the way I used to. It became apparent to me back then, when I was receiving help, that this was some sort of 'brushed under the carpet' issue that actually a heck of lot of other people were also experiencing. I am constantly overwhelmed with gratitude and praise for those that share their stories with me, and put their trust in my experience.

Anxiety can feel rubbish, and we're all human beings with life's rollercoaster testing us at every turn, but by reading this book, by learning about yourself, by being brave and asking for help, and accepting and letting go of the past, you *can* have a healthier, happier and anxiety-free future.

I am proof that this shouldn't define who you are, be strong, be you, be proud my friend, and welcome to the rest of your life ... it's an honour to share it with you.

Activity alert

This simple fun activity is one of my favourites. Now we're (hopefully) feeling more empowered and confident, let's cement that future with some visual evidence.

Take a big piece of card, canvas or paper, an app on your smartphone or tablet, or why not even a piece of wall if you have permission to decorate ... we're going to create your 'Future You'. ☉ Using magazines, mood board apps such as Pinterest, websites, etc. for inspiration, we're going to create a 'mood board' of where you're heading. We want to make this as detailed and vibrant as possible. ☉ Maybe you cut out and stick, or draw, or paint, or write, or 'cut and paste' ... whatever works for you, create your own visual representation of how the 'new you' is going to look and feel. Pictures, quotes, drawings, celebrities, places, feelings, aspirations ... whatever you find which fuels excitement and passion, pop it on your board. ☉ You can keep adding to this as time goes on, it can be permanently evolving, but ensure you pop your board somewhere where you can see it regularly, and allow yourself to 'be' what you create. ☉ By putting our desires out there and keeping a track on them, we give ourselves every chance to accomplish and realise them. Enjoy creating the future you want.

Dr Reetta says...
Talking, sharing and caring

Positive relationships and being able to connect with others is essential to mental wellbeing. Talking to and sharing with others can relieve tension and help you stay in good psychological health. It can help you clarify what your thoughts, feelings and main concerns are, and working out what you can do about them. Expressing emotions can build and strengthen your relationships, increase your sense of belonging and help you feel less alone.

Top tips for learning to share and express your feelings

Top tip 1
If you express your emotions, it can encourage people around you to do the same. It could start with the two simple words 'I feel ...'. Try it out when you are doing something together, rather than sitting down face to face – it feels less intimidating.

Top tip 2
Next time someone close to you says they are 'stressed' or 'so busy' (which most of us seem to be these days), encourage *them* to discuss their feelings – remember, we all have feelings! Try saying something supportive in response – 'it sounds like you've had a lot on' or 'that sounds really tough' – even this can help ease the load and help someone feel they're listened to and not alone.

Top tip 3
If talking feels too difficult, I agree with Anna, try sharing your feelings by writing them down. Keeping a diary or journal can help you deal with times of upset. You could be writing down your thoughts in a diary

▶

format, as if you were talking to a friend, or you could do it in a more creative or abstract way, perhaps writing down song lyrics, poetry, or short stories.

We're all different – and we all have different approaches when it comes to talking about personal difficulties. Some of us are very open, some are very guarded, the rest are somewhere in between. Have a think, where would you like to be on this spectrum? Where do your beliefs about talking come from? What were your experiences of expressing emotions or observing your family members do so when you were a child? It can be useful to think about talking as 'taking charge' of your situation, rather than something negative, such as a sign of weakness or a 'conversation killer'.

I feel privileged to hear about my clients' inner lives and anxieties. For someone to open up and let me hear their 'story' is often the beginning of the journey towards something better. Often the journey is about understanding the overwhelming feelings, learning to tolerate the uncertainties of life, accepting the imperfections, or developing new ways of dealing with things. Learning to talk about yourself and allowing others to witness your vulnerability can be life changing – as it has been for Anna. I often find myself thinking that if only people knew how common anxiety truly is, and that even the most confident or successful people can have these difficulties.

If you are thinking about talking to a professional, you are probably wondering whether it will help. Unfortunately there aren't clear-cut answers – there are too many factors that impact on the outcome for any given individual. However, there are tools that you can use to assess your levels of anxiety/distress and how motivated you might be to make changes in your life (for example, see the 'clients' section on www.supportingsafetherapy.org). Have a look at Anna's guidance on 'Who can I talk to?', and once you have chosen who it is, give it a go. It could make a really positive difference to you.

APPENDIX – CHILDREN AND ANXIETY

As a children's TV presenter for well over a decade, I have had a lot of communication and interaction with kids of all ages and from all walks of life. As a Childline counsellor, I have also heard from many young people over the years who need a safe trusted place to be listened to.

A lot of kids – nowadays in particular it seems – are reporting that they're feeling day-to-day anxiety and stress over a number of issues. School and parental pressure seems to come up a lot, as do friendship issues and self-esteem. We shouldn't ignore these pleas for help. Sometimes we might think 'what have kids got to worry about?' but in my professional and personal experience, children need as much support as possible to help them overcome any anxieties to ensure they have the best chance at a happy, carefree and supported future. The best thing we can all do is listen.

Dr Reetta shares here with you her Children's Anxiety Tool Kit, which is a really helpful resource for any trusted adult to read and implement should it ever be needed.

▶

Dr Reetta says...

If you are reading this book as a parent or carer, you can play an important role in helping your child learn the important life skill of managing anxiety. Firstly, I want to emphasise that children experience many fears and worries as part of typical development (e.g. separation anxiety around 12–18 months; fear of dark or particular animals around 2–4 years; and anxiety about social situations in adolescence). However, some children go on to develop symptoms that cause them a lot of distress and interfere with their day-to-day life. Symptoms to look out for are: feeling panicky/angry/irritable/tense, constant worrying, clinging, crying, tantrums, concentration difficulties, sleeping and eating difficulties, and complaining of feeling unwell (e.g. tummy aches, headaches, breathlessness).

I would always advise you to seek professional assessment, especially if your child's anxiety seems severe and is getting in the way of their day-to-day life at home and/or school. You can do this by speaking to your child's GP or school, who will be able to point you in the direction of your local NHS child mental health services. Alternatively, you can look for a private mental health professional, such as a clinical psychologist, who specialises in working with children. The British Psychological Society (BPS) website (http://www.bps.org.uk/bpslegacy/dcp) allows you to search for one near you.

In addition to support from professionals, there is a lot you can do to help your child. In my work with families, I support children and their parents to create their personal anxiety management 'toolkit'. This involves many of the same ideas that I have covered in this book for adults, but adapted to the child's age and developmental level. Some of these include:

Children's Anxiety Toolkit

• Helping your child become an expert on anxiety (remember, knowledge is power). This could be through self-help books, websites/online videos, or apps about anxiety.

▶

- Designing cards with coping statements (e.g. 'anxiety is just a bully, I can talk back to it!') and practising using these. Let's say your child is anxious about going to school – replacing the anxious thought with, 'I can do it, I will be ok' could help in reducing their anxiety.
- Learning about relaxation and breathing. There are many child-friendly resources out there, which can make this interesting and fun – just search online.
- Building a box of soothing items to help in an emotional emergency (ideally something to soothe all their senses, e.g. cuddly toy (touch), postcard from favourite holiday/photos of loved ones (vision) and a favourite snack (taste).
- Facing their fears with the help of a fear ladder (arranging fears from least scary to most scary) and learning that they can tolerate the anxiety as they climb up.

I always attempt to make the process of designing the toolkit creative (this could involve drawing, sticking, cutting pictures), with some 'fun' elements in it. I use a sheet of A4 or A3 paper and encourage the child to draw a picture of an actual toolkit. Once we have that as the base, I ask them to draw/write down all the different ways of coping with anxiety – which we would have by then discussed in our sessions. For example:

- The child could write down 'remember to use my deep breathing', or 'remember the video I watched about avoiding and how this makes my worries bigger'.
- Sometimes this means utilising the child's favourite toys/characters/TV programmes. For example, I have used LEGO mini figures to act out how to have more useful family conversations, and pictures of Disney princesses to think about ways of being brave and talking back to fears – and then writing down any ideas that come from these scenarios.
- It's handy having as many different tools as possible, as most children will end up saying 'it doesn't work!' when suggested to use a particular tool while anxious.

▶

- Remember, many of these tools are likely to involve you in some way. It could be that you need to prompt your child to use a particular tool, or the tool is about setting regular 1:1 talking time, or problem solving together.

Finally, don't underestimate the power of learning through observation – your child learning from watching you, and copying how you cope with anxiety and stress. What does your child see you doing when you are stressed out? Have you noticed that when you are stressed you shout more, or shut down emotionally? Have a think: is there something (be realistic here, us parents are only human!) that you could do differently? Could you express your emotions, in an age-appropriate way, so that your child understands how you are feeling? This could also be an ideal opportunity to teach your child about the importance of self-care by allowing yourself to step out from a situation or sitting down for a moment. In addition, times of stress could be an opportunity to teach your child about different people's viewpoints, how to make amends after an argument or something else that comes up about relationships.

As a parent, pay attention to your own emotions when you are trying to calm down your distressed child – your child is likely to sense how you are feeling through your body language and tone of voice. Use a calm and soothing voice while acknowledging how they are feeling, rather than asking them to calm down or telling them they will be fine. You can teach your child that emotions don't last forever, they come and go. Even the hardest ones, like anxiety and fear, will eventually pass.

Let's say your daughter or son worries about being separated from you. Instead of dismissing the worry and telling them it'll be ok, you could try naming the feelings and help your child to talk through what it is that is upsetting them. Perhaps you could plan a special goodbye ritual or your child could keep an item of yours to remind them of you during the time you are apart. You could also try to focus them on how you look forward to spending some time together in the garden/on the sofa/in the park after school.

RESOURCES

Anxiety UK
www.anxietyuk.org.uk / Telephone: 08444 775 774
Charity providing support for anyone affected by anxiety.

CALM (Campaign Against Living Miserably for men aged 15–35)
www.thecalmzone.net / Telephone: 0800 58 58 58
National charity working to prevent male suicide in the UK, with a
helpline and a webchat service. The helpline is for men who need to talk
or find information and support. They are open 5pm–midnight, 365 days
a year.

Mind
www.mind.org.uk / Telephone: 0300 123 3393
Mind believe no one should face a mental health problem alone. The
charity listen, give support and advice and will fight your corner. They
believe in empowering anyone dealing with a mental health problem.

The Prince's Trust
www.princes-trust.org.uk / Telephone: 0800 842 842
The Prince's Trust helps young people ages 13–30 to get into jobs,
education and training. The Trust prides itself on giving second chances
and support to disadvantaged young people who have perhaps
struggled with mental health issues, homelessness or perhaps been in
trouble with the law. They are a hugely positive charity who can help
change lives.

Samaritans
www.samaritans.org / Telephone: 116 123 (UK)
National charity that provides 24/7 support to anyone in distress. You
can call, text, email, write or meet with them face to face, off the
record – see website for contact details. You don't have to be suicidal to
contact them.

Websites for finding a therapist

BACP

www.bacp.co.uk

The British Association for Counselling and Psychotherapy (BACP) provide a register of counsellors and psychotherapists accredited by the Professional Standards Authority for Health and Social Care.

BPS

www.bps.org.uk

British Psychological Society provide a directory of Chartered Psychologists.

ACKNOWLEDGEMENTS

Anna Williamson

Without the support and belief of several people, this book probably would not have been anything but a whimsical pipe dream.

I have such thanks and gratitude to my incredible editor Charlotte Croft and the whole team at Bloomsbury Publishing, whose expertise, encouragement and vision have been invaluable – the very best publishing house a girl could wish for!

Psychologist extraordinaire (and super mum) Dr Reetta Newell, who I just knew was perfect for the book, and shared my vision re helping anxiety sufferers, and whose contribution and expert advice has been the icing on the cake – with a cherry on top!

My agent Samantha, my wing woman, who encouraged me to share my experiences with you in the first place, brought Bloomsbury and me together as a dream team, and who without this book wouldn't have come to fruition. Claire 'Mulvers', my loyal pal and publicist, who has never let me down, and who now knows way too much about me!

A heartfelt thank you to my loving family, particularly Mum and Dad, who have never judged me, always supported me, kept my feet firmly on the ground, and who have helped shape the person I am today. Proof that love and a good cuddle can conquer all.

My fabulous friends, you all know who you are. For never giving up on me no matter how flaky and frustrating I might have been, and for being my confidantes for life. You're my rocks.

Thanks to my husband Alex, my 'A Team-mate'. For always understanding and accepting me and my aspirations, for encouraging me to keep going when 'writer's block' threatened, and for believing in me and this book wholeheartedly. A special mention to our little 'Hercy', who at the time of writing this has accompanied me the whole nine months of putting this book together, from the comfort of my tummy – every kick, punch and hiccup has kept Mummy company during even the most solitary of hours.

A big thank you to all at Mind, Childline and The Prince's Trust – I'm super proud to be an ambassador and spokesperson for three incredible charities. A special mention to Sophie Rawlings, Paul Farmer and the team at Mind for your help with this book, and whose work in the mental health arena has been, and continues to be, life changing for so many suffering with anxiety, and all areas of mental health.

And last, but certainly not least, the biggest high-five goes to you, and every fellow anxiety sufferer. Thank you, and well done for picking up my book and wanting to learn more about something which is experienced by so many, yet talked about by so few. To all my inspirational clients, fans and followers, I really am blessed to be welcomed into your lives, and I am honoured to welcome you into mine.

Reetta Newell

I feel privileged to have worked with many clients, colleagues and supervisors over the years who have helped shape me as a clinical psychologist. I would like to thank my two beautiful daughters for keeping me grounded with their love and cheekiness, and my husband for all his support.

INDEX

Janet ⸻⸻ ⸻or of the Stephanie Plum series, the Lizzy and Diesel series, twelve romance novels, the Alexandra Barnaby novels and Trouble Maker graphic novels, and *How I Write: Secrets of a Bestselling Author*.

Lee Goldberg is a screenwriter, TV producer, and the author of several books, including *King City*, *The Walk*, and the bestselling *Monk* series of mysteries. He has earned two Edgar Award nominations and was the 2012 recipient of the Poirot Award from Malice Domestic.

Praise for Janet Evanovich's bestselling novels:

'Janet Evanovich's characters are eccentric and exaggerated, the violence often surreal and the plot dizzily speedy: but she produces as many laughs as anyone writing crime today' *The Times*

'Janet Evanovich's madcap comic mystery is pure, classic farce' *New York Times Book Review*

'Evanovich's series of New Jersey comedy thrillers are among the great joys of contemporary crime fiction . . . all the easy class and wit that you expect to find in the best American TV comedy, but too rarely find in modern fiction' *GQ*

'An engaging mix of slapstick, steam and suspense' *People*

'Reads like the screen-play for a 1930s screwball comedy: fast, funny and furious . . . The rollicking plot . . . keeps the reader breathless' *Publishers Weekly*

'Undeniably funny' *Scotsman*

'Romantic and gripping, this novel is an absolute tonic' *Good Housekeeping*

'The pace never flags, the humour is grandly surreal, and the dialogue fairly sizzles off the page' *Irish Times*

'Non-stop laughs with plenty of high jinks' *USA Today*